Kid Trillionaire

Question: What comes after a trillion?

Answer: I don't know, but don't tell Congress!

Kid Trillionaire

How a Little Kid Can Make a Big Fortune

John Louzonis, Age 13

Einstein Blueprint Press

Published by Einstein Blueprint Press, Manhattan, New York.

Printed in the United States of America

10 9 8 7 6 5 4 3 2 1

ISBN-13: 978-0692121535
ISBN-10: 0692121536

This book is dedicated to my parents, Daniel and Inez Louzonis, who have been so supportive of my personal Kid Trillionaire journey.

TABLE OF CONTENTS

ABOUT THE AUTHOR

John Anthony Louzonis was born in 2004 in Charlotte, North Carolina. He's bounced around a lot since - living in both Newton and Cohasset in Massachusetts, Manhasset, New York, London (UK), and now lives in downtown Manhattan – right next to the World Trade Center.

John started algebra at age 5, had read all the Harry Potter books by 6, and began calculus at age 7. John is also a piano whiz and a chess champion having won a few major tournaments in the hyper-competitive NYC area.

John can do almost anything on the computer. He landed his first web design client when he was only 10. His client work now includes graphic design, podcast production, editing, and transcription. John also runs email and social media marketing campaigns, builds funnels, sales pages, and membership sites for other businesses.

It's best to connect with John on LinkedIn. You can find out more about John's education by visiting **EinsteinBlueprint.com/John**.

CHAPTER 1

WHY SHOULD KIDS GET RICH NOW?

There are so many reasons why a kid should try to make money. I could write this entire book on just why. But instead, I am dedicating one chapter to it. For starters, a kid who's banking dough can:

Buy Stuff

What do you think your wardrobe would look like if you had hundreds of dollars pouring in? Or your toy closet. Do you think your Nerf Gun collection would only have the tiny little pistols if you were rolling in the dough? Or would it have the Vulcan pouring out 3 darts a second?

If you were making lots of money, would you go to the movie theater and starve while the rich kids next to you eat massive, $14 tubs of inorganic popcorn? Of course not!

If you have lots of money, you can buy anything you want without worrying about it costing too much!

When you are rich, you can buy the new $1,200 iPhone X. You can get the super pricey drone that lets you drop water balloons at people from 30 ft above. You can buy $7 Unicorn Frappuccinos that taste like rainbow barf. You can show off your $900 Gucci handbag that cost $2 to make by some poor kid in Thailand. And when you are 16, you can buy your very own car. You can go buy plane tickets to Disney.

You're probably like, "Shut up and tell me how to make money!" But there are many more reasons for becoming rich than just this. For example, you will gain:

Respect

What do you think life in school would be like if the bullies saluted as you walked by?

Or if the teacher was scared to give you detention because you're like a mini-king on campus?

How would it feel if the so-called cool kids wanting to hang out with you, instead of the other way around? That's what it will be like in school, when you are rich.

When you have money, no one is going to talk behind your back about you. Well, they will, but they'll be saying, "I wish I had his/her clothes, and his/her iPhone X-Plus," and so on.

By the way, Michael Dell earned more money in high school than his economics teacher. How do you think that made the teacher feel?

When you are rich, there is an aura around you. An air of respect. If you don't believe me, look at the richest kids in your school. Does anyone really mess with them? Do they get shoved in their lockers? Probably not. Even if buying stuff and the respect that comes with being rich were all the benefits, you would still want to be rich. But wait, there's more…

Self-Confidence

How would it feel to go to the local illegal poker ring run by the high schoolers, and not worry if you lose $100?

But what if you could totally bomb a test and not even feel upset? Why? Because you are filthy rich! If somebody is mean to you, you don't care at all!

When you have money falling out of your pockets, you'll feel bulletproof. After all, you're the man/woman! You can afford to go to Six Flags with your friends and blow money on all those rip-off games!

You got rich, you can do anything! You'll tackle that hard rope course or that cool skate trick because you won't be afraid to fail! Nothing is off-limits! There's also the...

Position of Power

How would it feel to not have to wait until Christmas or your birthday to get something you want? Or if you want some candy, not having to wait until Halloween? When you are rich, you rise to a position of power. Nothing controls or constrains you.

Christmas in July can be a thing! Or Halloween every month! When you are rich, you can make your own holiday calendar. But there's more. If your parents can't afford to go to Disney, you can help pay for some of it! Suddenly, you are going to Disney - maybe with those express passes that let you cut the line! This is one of the best parts of being rich!

Control Destiny

One day, your idiot little brother decides it's a good idea to use your Xbox as a place to put his glass of juice, and he spills it all over the place, ruining your Xbox. Now you can't play Call of Doody. (I know it's misspelled. I can do what I want, I'm rich.)

When you are rich, you can just buy a new Xbox! You should also make your brother work for you and repay off the $200 bucks he owes you, plus $100 of interest for wasting your time.

But the point is, you can buy a new Xbox and have your thirst for Call of Doody satisfied. You didn't have to deal with not having an Xbox and your brother going unpunished because "he's only 3". If you weren't rich, then you might have to wait a really long time to get a new Xbox - if ever. You are in control of when you get what you want.

And maybe your parents want you to be a dentist. But you don't want to be a local figure of fear. If you are a millionaire, you can tell your parents, "I don't want to torture kids! I'm a millionaire! I'm going to be whatever I want!"

Massive Head Start

If you make a ton of money as a kid, you will have a massive head start over everyone else. You can use whatever you make as a kid to launch your future ventures. Warren Buffett had $68,000 (in today's money) when he was 14. That's more than most adults have today! Think of how much that helped him later in life.

When he was fifteen, he and one of his buddies bought a used pinball machine. Then they went to a barbershop and said, "If we put this machine in here, customers can play it while waiting, and we'll split the profits." Soon Buffett did this multiple times. He then sold the business to a war veteran for about $15,000 (in today's money).

He might not have been able to buy the pinball machine and do what he did if he hadn't made money at a young age. So it helps to get rich and have a head start. Have you ever played that "Temple Run" game? You know how at the beginning you can buy a head start? Well, getting rich is like hitting that button. (But somehow that darn monkey thing catches up anyway...)

Margin For Error

One of most important reasons for trying to get rich right now is that you have a wide margin for error.

Right now, you don't have a family to feed, rent to pay, and all sorts of other responsibilities that you will have when you grow up. So you can afford to mess up now. If you lose $100 on a failed fidget spinner business, then it's not the end of the world. It's not like the IRS is going to bust down your door because you can't pay taxes. But in the future, when you have a spouse and kids, failure will come with far more consequences. This is why most adults are afraid to quit their jobs and take new chances to improve their career.

But if you make money now, you'll have money in the bank that you can play with, without worrying about paying any bills - maybe ever! It's like having an extra parachute when you jump off a plane! So get rich now, because this is the best time!

Popularity

Who's popular in school, the rich kids with the iPhone X-Plus and all the cool swag, or the poor kids who have flip phones and clothes from the Goodwill store? (How embarrassing.) It's definitely the rich kids. Obviously, when you become rich, you become a cool rich kid. But in a way, you are even cooler than those other kids, because they got it all from their parents, while you pulled it out of thin air. They'll be begging to hang out with you. Now the tables have turned, haven't they?

You'll also be cooler in high school and college, as well. You can be the cool kid who hosts massive dorm parties! And if you're rich, you won't have to get a job. You can move to Japan or retire to the beach in the Hamptons. Wherever you go, you will be as cool as a cucumber.

Independence

Did you know 35% of Americans are dependent on the government for money and food? What would happen if the government stopped paying or ran out of money? People would starve! And how embarrassing would it be to be dependent on handouts? I imagine that it is very.

Did you know that 33% of millennials (people aged 18-34) live with their parents? How embarrassing that must be to tell your girlfriend/boyfriend, "Come over to my place." and take her/him to your parents' house and then down to your little corner of the basement.

So when you are rich, you don't need your parents or the government to support you. You can take care of yourself.

Less Stress

You're short, you've got pimples, the cafeteria food is nasty, your homework is boring and hard....you've got a whole lot on your plate. You don't need any more anxiety in your life. Yet it piles on like the green beans at lunch.

But when you have money, you'll feel taller. The pimples will shrink away. The cafeteria food will taste better. (Somehow.) Your homework will be less painful. This will all happen once you make money. I promise.

Become Happier

Money isn't happiness. There are many people who are millionaires but their relationships are wrecks. Just look at the celebrities in the tabloids.

However, is it happier to worry about how to pay the bills, or to relax because everything is taken care of? I think it's happier to relax.

Is it happier to stay in one place your whole life because you're poor, or to travel around the whole world? I think traveling is more fun.

Is it happier to get kicked out of your house because you couldn't pay the mortgage, or be in control of your home... and your life? I think I would like to be in control.

But remember, true happiness comes from people, not things. Man, I sound like a Disney movie.

Become Attractive

Ladies, who would you rather date? A poor guy who always smells like pee and hasn't shaved for seven months and is fat because he can't afford vegan-organic green smoothies, or a rich guy who smells like flowers (or the most expensive Axe body spray), is clean, handsome, and strong? I'm guessing that most would say the second guy. Rich people are just more attractive, thanks to the plastic surgery.

But really, there is something about wealthy people that just is very magnetic. Maybe it's the money. Maybe it's the fact that they've done things that others can only talk trash about. Whatever it is, people like it. If you start making money now, people will start looking at you in a whole new light. You can make yourself look 10 times more amazing with money. So make some cash and find your soulmate. Man, I sound like a perfume commercial.

You Can Help People!

When you are rich, not only will money change your life, it will give you the ability to change others' lives.

Maybe you feel bad for the starving kids in New Jersey. And Africa too, I guess. When you are rich, you can send them donations so they can get food and water! My family sponsors (pays for food and water for) 3 families in Africa. This is really cliché, but it feels great to get cards from the kids and see a picture of them with the goat that they were able to buy with our support.

So don't forget to give back when you make money. After all, not everyone is rich like you.

Future Success

If you get rich right now, you'll be building a solid foundation for many more successes. Maybe that big company will be more inclined to hire you as CEO if you made your first million in high school. Or maybe your future businesses will be better funded, thus allowing them to grow more, making you even more money.

Everyone who has become extremely wealthy on their own has used their first success, no matter how small, to build bigger and bigger successes on.

When you get rich, you create all sorts of opportunities for yourself. Maybe even a business that is expensive to start is possible for you! Or maybe you can take your pre-made thank you card business international!

So make money now, so you can make even more money later.

Because You Can

The famous mountaineer George Mallory, who attempted to climb Mt. Everest, was asked why he wanted to climb it before he tried to. He replied, "Because it's there!" And that is the best reason why you should get rich now. Because you can. You can overcome poverty (like only $80 a month for allowance) and sadness (you crashed your $1,500 drone) if you get rich! So what are you waiting for?

Those are just some of the most inarguable reasons why you should make money now. You're probably like, "Well, yeah I want to get rich, but can I? I'm just a kid." It's possible for sure. Just turn the page if you don't believe me.

CHAPTER 2

OH YEAH, IT'S POSSIBLE!

I want you to know that it is possible to get rich as a kid. There are so many stories of kids getting rich, and I am going to share a couple to inspire you.

Caleb Maddix

Caleb Maddix got his start at 13, when he wrote his first book, *Keys For Success For Kids*. Hey, I'm 13 and I am writing my first book, what a coincidence!

But since then, Caleb has been making a ton of money speaking. To all of you motor-mouths out there, yes, you can make money talking. A ton of it, too. Caleb makes $20,000 in a single hour by just speaking at an event. He generally talks at schools and business conferences, motivating and inspiring people.

He is 15 years old and worth one million dollars, and that number is only going up. Go check him out!

Palmer Luckey

Palmer Luckey started tinkering with Virtual Reality headsets during his teenage years. To fund this hobby, Palmer worked many odd jobs, such as fixing cell phones. He made over $36,000 by doing things like that. This little hobby led him to develop the Oculus Rift, a VR headset. When the Rift started to receive attention, Palmer dropped out of college and started working on the Rift full time. As the Rift became more and more successful, Palmer started to make more and more money.

In 2014, Facebook bought Palmer's company for $2 BILLION! So maybe you tinker with gadgets. You could become the next Palmer Luckey.

EvanTube

When Evan was 9 years old, he and his dad started making YouTube videos of them reviewing toys. They didn't expect to make money off of it, but as it got more and more popular, they started to make money off of the videos by putting ads on them, getting sponsorships, and using something called an affiliate link. An affiliate link is a special link to Amazon where you could buy the toy and Evan would get some of the money.

Now, they make about $1.3 million a year! Just by reviewing toys and playing some video games! Now that's what I call a dream job. Now before you convince your parents to go and buy you a ton of toys to review, remember that you need to do something to make your videos special. Maybe you could review different types of toys to make yourself unique. When making money, you always have to differentiate yourself from the crowd.

Emily Shai

Emily really liked to have sleepovers and wanted to make a little bit of money. What did she do? She wrote an 80-page book about sleepovers and sold it door-to-door. The end result? She earned over $20,000. And she was only 10 years old! The book is called 5 Steps To The Perfect Sleepover, if you are interested. Heck, she inspired me to write this book.

Since then, Emily has started a mission to help 2,000 kids write a book. Learn from Emily. She proved you can make money from anything, even sleepovers.

Emerson Spartz

Emerson Spartz was just 12 years old when he started MuggleNet.com, which was for many years the number one Harry Potter fan site. It was a huge success, and Emerson earned around $100,000 a year.

Around 2009, Spartz started a couple more companies, before starting another site called Spartz Media, which helped businesses with social media. Spartz later changed the name of the business to Dose. Spartz got his start by making a website on something he was obsessed about. Maybe you really like a book or a TV series. You can make money off of that!

Ashley Qualls

Ashley Qualls started a website called whateverlife.com, which provided free HTML (a coding language) tutorials and MySpace layouts. What is MySpace, you ask? The social media website that came before Facebook. Absolutely nobody goes on it anymore.

But when Ashley launched her site, she made $70,000 in her first few months! After MySpace went the way of the dinosaurs, Ashley changed her website to a "hangout" for "alternative" millennials. What does that even mean? Does an alternative millennial only look at their phone 99% of the time? But Ashley had earned over $1 MILLION by the time she was 17.

So what's the lesson? MySpace was popular at the time, so Ashley profited off of it. Make money off of things that are currently popular!

Juliette Brindak

When Juliette was 10, she drew a set of characters called "Cool Girls". Later, Juliette took those "Cool Girls" and made a website based off of them called Miss O and Friends, an all-girl site for tweens.

What was a simple little project quickly became popular. Soon it would be the 3rd largest girls-only website. Now, Miss O and Friends is worth $15 million. Pretty impressive, huh? But who would have thought she could have made that much money off of a bunch of drawings?

Nick D'Aloisio

Nick was a 15-year-old computer nerd who made an app called Trimit. Trimit would take anything and summarize it. Great for school reports.

But it wasn't that lucrative, until the Chinese multi-billionaire Li Ka-Shing became interested in Trimit and gave Nick $300,000 in funding. Nick used the money to redesign the app. He also renamed it Summly.

When Summly was first released, over 250,000 people installed it. This attracted Yahoo's attention, and they bought the app for $30 MILLION dollars. Now Nick is filthy rich.

Are you a computer nerd? Maybe you can make something like Summly.

Isabella Taylor

Isabella was just 10 years old when she started designing clothes. Since then, she's been featured in many magazines such as Forbes, Seventeen, and Elle. Isabella has appeared on FOX, CNN, and MSNBC. She's even partnered with Dell to present her Fall collection during New York Fashion Week.

Isabella also has spoken at TEDx multiple times. (TEDx is a conference where people speak about Technology, Entertainment, and Design.) Don't tell your parents about Isabella, because they'll say, "Why aren't you like her?"

So there you have it. A 15-year-old making money and getting invited to TV shows and conferences left and right. Why can't you do that? If you have a flair for fashion, you could do something like what she does.

David Karp

David Karp was just 14 when he began interning for Frederator Studios, an animation company. He dropped out of high school one year later to work on little side projects. Later, David started working with UrbanBaby, an online parenting form. When UrbanBaby was bought by CNET, David left it and started Davidville, a company where he would build websites for people.

While working on Davidville, Karp started Tumblr, a website that let people make "tumbleblogs", short blogs. Eventually, David renamed Davidville to Tumblr, Inc. and stopped the website design and worked on Tumblr full-time. In 2013, Yahoo bought Tumblr for $1.1 BILLION! Karp now has $200 million. The moral of the story? Hard work and constant innovation will take you places.

Thomas Suarez

When Thomas was 9, he learned how to code. Ever since then, he's been making tons of apps and games. His most famous game is hilarious. It's called Bustin Jieber, and it's basically Whac-a-Mole with Justin Bieber instead of a mole. Since then, he's made Wi-Tag, which is Laser Tag on your phone.

He also gave a TEDx talk when he was in 6th Grade. Since then, it's become one of the most viewed TEDx talks of all time!

So there you have it. You can make money off of a game where you whack Justin Bieber!

Chris Owens

Chris was 14 years old when he launched his first business: Mac Bundle Box. The idea was simple. You buy the Bundle Box, and you would get all sorts of useful Mac programs for a fraction of the usual price. He would buy the programs from the developer at a discount. Mac Bundle Box made Chris a millionaire at 16!

But he also started another business, Branchr, which is an advertising business that makes ads for phones and tablets. He said, "I don't know where I will be in 10 years time but I won't leave Branchr until it has reached £100 million."

Yes, it is possible to make a million pounds (British money) at 16! Chris is proof of that!

Leanna Archer

Leanna was just 9 years old when she started her business, a line of all-natural hair products. She used her grandmother's recipe to make the shampoo, and before she turned it into a business, her friends were asking her what she used in her hair, and she gave them some. Before you knew it, people throwing money at her for some more of it. At that point she started selling it to anyone who asked. But then she got interviewed in a newspaper when she was 11 and her business has grown massively! She now sells her products in over 80 countries!

So let that be a lesson. You could make a ton of money off of Grandma's secret cookie recipe! Though it might not be so secret afterwards...

Robert Nay

Robert was 14 years old when his friends suggested making an iPhone app. So Robert went to the library, did some ol' fashioned book learning, and made an app, Bubble Ball, a physics game. Believe it or not, this app was downloaded 2 MILLION TIMES within its first two weeks of being released! It even became the number 1 most popular game in iTunes, knocking Angry Birds off its perch! (Pun intended.)

He started a company, Nay Games, which has made 3 other apps as well. Robert's advice to kids is, "You can do amazing things if you just try."

How NOT To Make Money

While there are many things you can do to make money, some of them you shouldn't do. Really anything dishonest or against the law. Here are some examples. Selling fireworks is not a great idea, because some kid is going to blow off his fingers and make you feel horrible. Don't gamble, because you have no guaranteed chance of winning, and you could get in huge trouble. Doing other kids' homework is a bad idea. One kid near where I live would take the SAT for people.

Scamming people is dishonest and bad for your health, as countless con artists have gotten beaten to a pulp by angry victims. Selling drugs is probably the stupidest thing you could ever do. Do that, and you'll be packing your bags for juvie. All these ideas are just dumb. But people do them. Don't be the idiot who actually got sent to juvie because instead of selling candy in school, you sold drugs. Like I said, if you think it is unethical or it's against the law(duh), don't do it.

Wanna know another way not to make money? This might burst your bubble, but playing sports is not a good way to get rich. Did you know that 36.2 million kids play in organized sports? Guess what? Every single one of them wants to be in the pro leagues, just like you. You might be a fantastic player. But there is someone even better. According to a study done by Michigan State college, the odds of a high school football player making it to the NFL is 1 in 6,000! For the MLB, the odds are 1 in 4,000! Worst of all are the odds for the NBA: 1 in 10,000!

And even if you do make it on a pro team, apparently 78% of pro athletes go broke within 5 years of retiring.

My Dad said he wasted his entire childhood playing basketball, hoping to go pro. According to that study, he only had a one-in-10,000 chance of making it. So that's why it kills me when all the kids I know just want to become pro sports players. There's nothing wrong with playing sports for fun, but don't bet everything on going pro, okay?

And you can forget trying to be the next PewDiePie or something. Seriously, there are 100 hours of content uploaded to YouTube every minute. Why would your MINECRAFFT LET'S PLAY + INSANE PvP + AMAZON GIVEAWAY + APPLE GIVEAWAY + BITCON GIVEAWAY actually make money compared to the other quality videos being uploaded?

It's totally possible to make lots of dough as a kid, and these kids have proven it. Now it is your turn. So go out there and get rich!

CHAPTER 3

FOLLOWING THE CROWD WILL MAKE YOU POOR

"Whenever you find yourself on the side of the majority, it is time to pause and reflect." - Mark Twain

If you want to succeed and rise above the crowd in anything, you simply can't do what everyone else is doing.

You can't go where everyone else goes, think what everyone else thinks, value what everyone else values, do what everyone else does, because then you'll end up with the same results as everyone else. You may not become broke, but you won't ever be rich, and you won't ever have the *Trillionaire* lifestyle.

There are actually many subtle, dangerous ways that kids succumb to peer pressure that don't involve doing drugs or other obvious negative activities. I'm going to break them down in this chapter.

Don't Rely on School

If you get good grades, all your dreams will come true - so they say. Sure, subjects like history, science, and math are an important part of a traditional education. But there are many other skills that are needed for success in real life that are not covered in school. Like making money. Duh.

I'll bet barely any, maybe one or two at best, of your classmates think directly about making money. The rest of them are focused on academics and getting good grades, because their parents and teachers have convinced them that those are the most important things - also because that's what everyone else is focused on.

But the reality is, the most financially successful people on Earth have had little to no formal education, in fact, many of them struggled tremendously in school. Some have even flunked out altogether! I have provided many examples in this book, and you can easily find many more online by searching for "famous dropouts".

School doesn't even teach the basics about business, entrepreneurship, economics, or personal finance. Nor do kids in classrooms acquire any real marketable skills, like salesmanship or computer programming.

School doesn't encourage kids to take risks. Take a risk in school, you might be laughed at by your former friends, or even end up in the principal's office!

Quit Wasting Time

> *"Hard work pays off in the future. Laziness pays off now."*
> *- internet*

The average teenager somehow figures out how to get 9 hours of screen time a day in. If they were coding, or creating the next Windows operating system like a young Bill Gates, that would be one thing. But they're probably watching cat videos and Logan Paul. They're all wasting tons of time and massive opportunities to start making money.

There's nothing wrong with playing a game here and there. But doing it to those levels is a formula for guaranteed failure in many areas of life.

Wasting time doing unproductive things cements bad habits. It gets harder and harder to quit. Before you know it, you'll wake up with 3 gray hairs on your bald head and realize that you've spent thousands of hours watching movies, reality TV, and other people playing video games.

When you waste time, I guarantee you will regret it one day. Time is your most valuable resource. Period. The whole point of making money is so you can have more time. There is nobody on Earth who can just pay $100 for another day. Every second spent playing Fortnite is gone forever. Poof.

If you want to be a *Kid Trillionaire*, you have to value your time. When you're making money, you want to minimize the time that you work, and maximize the money that you make.

Never Settle For Dead End Jobs

> *"A dead-end job is a job in which there is little or no chance of career development and advancement into a higher paid position." - Wikipedia*

There's nothing wrong with flipping burgers or shoveling horse manure. There're lessons to be learned from every job - even if it's just how to hold your breath for two hours straight. By the way, my Dad apparently shoveled horse manure for one of his jobs when he was in high school, LOL.

On any job, even a dead-end job, you can learn things like how to show up on time, follow directions, and deliver fantastic customer service. It's way better than spending all day watching a video about the Kardashians. After all, you get paid. But once you've learned all you can, it's time to move on and create better work for yourself.

I do have this one job where I transcribe podcasts. It's definitely dead-end, but it pays well, it's pretty simple, and I'm learning a ton about voice technology, the subject of the podcasts.

People like dead-end jobs because it's easy, guaranteed work. They trade away their dreams for what they think is job security. Dead-end jobs should only be used as stepping stones to better jobs, and eventually, the ultimate job.

The ultimate job is no job. It's called being an entrepreneur. Anyone who is in charge of a business is an entrepreneur. You should not be calling anyone "boss". You want to be working for yourself. When you are an entrepreneur, you give yourself a paycheck. You get to keep as much money as you make.

Become Financially Literate

Most people just don't understand money. They don't know how to earn it, they don't know how to spend it, and they don't know how to save it. Apparently, 62% of American adults have less than $1,000 in their savings account. Even I have more than that in my PayPal alone. I think my 11 year old sister has that much under her mattress too.

Meet Bankrupt Betty. She personifies financial illiteracy. She spends every single penny she gets on designer clothing and $5 Starbucks lattes. She borrows money from unsuspecting people all the time. When she does actually have a few dollars in her pocket, she also foolishly lends money to shysters even more irresponsible than her! Betty gets overcharged at stores and restaurants and doesn't realize it because she doesn't count her change. She doesn't understand the concept of a budget. Savings, you ask? What savings?

Bankrupt Betty just doesn't understand that you can't spend more than you earn. She's just doing what everyone else does, so it must be okay, right?

Wrong. She and her friends, also broke, are just like 65% of America. If there was one rule for never becoming poor, then it's to not spend more than you earn. It's simple math and undeniable logic. If you make a billion dollars a year, but spend two billion dollars a year, then you are going to be one billion dollars in the hole.

All you have to do to distance yourself from Betty and the crowd is learn the basics, the ABCs of financial literacy by using common sense.

Never Gamble

> *"Lottery: A tax on people who are bad at math." - Ambrose Bierce*

My grandpa once had a scratch ticket and I told him that - that the lottery is a tax on people who were bad at math - and he snapped at me! I think I was 7 years old but I had read the quote on the wall at a funky burrito joint in Naples, Florida.

American adults spent $73 BILLION on lottery tickets in 2017. Obviously, gambling is widespread and accepted as normal.

The crowd is full of suckers prone to get-rich-quick-schemes. The appeal of lazy, work-free riches is just too irresistible to most people NO MATTER how many times they get burned.

Once, my great-grandmother told my Dad that she had just won $500 from a slot machine! My Dad asked her how much she put in. She wouldn't answer him. He asked her again, and she finally said, "Never mind about that!" It's anyone's guess to how much she spent. But if I was a gambling man, I'd bet it was way more than the $500 she supposedly "won".

The crowd doesn't just play the lottery. They bet on sports ($100 billion per year). They get robbed by slot machines at casinos ($400 billion industry). Then there's also online gambling…

Did you know that millennials in 2017 bought a ton of Bitcoin on their credit cards? No wonder the price of it exploded so high….before crashing to bits.

If you want to be a *Kid Trillionaire*, never gamble with your money. They say you can never win if you don't play. Well, you can't lose if you don't play either! You shouldn't ever rely on random chance.

Never Stop Learning

> *"When you stop learning, you start dying." - Albert Einstein*

Most kids are conditioned to think that learning only happens in a certain time and a certain place - school. So when they are outside of the classroom, they stop reading, writing, creating, focusing, and thinking. They totally shut their brains down. It would be fine if they learned how to make money at school, but as I mentioned earlier, they don't.

Your mind is a muscle. It withers and dies if you don't exercise it. The crowd turns off their brains outside of school. After college, they don't read or write at all! 40% of people never read another book after college!

By doing that, they kill all sorts of opportunities for themselves. They never learn new skills, like coding. They close their minds to new ideas. In this crazy world, where there are new things all the time, you have to always keep learning. Otherwise, you'll get destroyed by the competition.

Lose the Victim Card

> *"It's always easy to blame others. You can spend your entire life blaming the world, but your successes or failures are entirely your own." - Paulo Coelho*

Meet Paula. She went to college, majored in fun, and came out $50,000 in the hole. So what does Paula do? She goes to a protest and blames the government for not paying for her college. The government laughed.

What does Paula do? She starts working at McDonald's but constantly moans about how her job is "demeaning". Excuse me for a second, but who pointed a gun at her head and forced her to go work at McDonalds? She thinks her parents should pay off her student loans AND pay for her cell phone, her clothes, and her rent.

When Paula gets her first payday, she immediately spends the entire check on Powerball tickets. None of them win, quite surprisingly! After all, the odds were 292 million to 1 AGAINST her winning. She complains about how terrible her luck is. Paula gets fired from McDonalds for "insufficient enthusiasm" and "taking selfies, not orders." Paula whines some more and blames her cousin for encouraging her to get the job in the first place.

Paula somehow manages to get a desk job at ABC Enterprises. It's not long before she's complaining about her coworkers and the quality of the free coffee and donuts. She gets fired after posting on Tumblr, "OMG my boss, like, sucks! He's such a jerk! And Steve always smells like a sewer!"

Listening to "Financial Guru Mernie Badoff", Paula maxes out her credit cards to invest in Badoff Funds, despite warnings from various family members. Badoff Funds is a scam, and she loses all of her borrowed money. She blames her family members for not warning her enough.

What happens now? Does Paula realize her poor life choices are the reason why she's broke? Nope! She blames the person sitting across from in her in High School English. Why? Who honestly knows? And the only people who will hear her complain are her 17 fake Tumblr followers.

Do you see what's going on here? Paula will never be rich because she will always blame other people for her troubles. Blaming other people (or "bad luck") will never make you any money! So don't be like Paula. When something bad happens to you, instead, figure out what went wrong, figure out what you can learn from the experience, and don't let it happen to you again.

It's Time to Lead!

"The first person you lead is yourself..." - various

As you can see, if you want to become a *Kid Trillionaire*, you can't follow the crowd.

You must take personal responsibility for everything in your life. You must become a voracious lifelong learner. You must angle for better and better job opportunities. You must value your money and time and also not assume school is going to make you rich.

Instead of following the crowd, you must lead the crowd. When Warren Buffett gives advice, people listen. He's a leader. He's worth $84.6 BILLION! Nobody in the crowd doing what everyone else does is worth $80 billion, forget $1 billion. But he has all sorts of fans who try to do exactly what he does.

There you have it. That's why you can't follow the crowd. Next, we're going to learn how you can start your *Kid Trillionaire* journey right now!

CHAPTER 4

START NOW!

You're probably thinking, "I want to get rich. But John, but how do I start?" Well, first of all, you have to know a little bit about making money.

Don't worry, there are tons of easy, free, and fun ways you can start to learn how to make money.

Stalk Mentors

Maybe you know someone who made him/herself rich. That's awesome, because then all of their wisdom is available to you. I'm sure they would be happy to teach you about making money.

This is a really efficient way to learn about making money, and countless entrepreneurs have had mentors like this. So find a family member, family friend, or neighbor who has made money, and learn as much as you can from them.

Research Like Crazy

There is this amazing thing called Google. With it, you can learn anything about almost everything. In an instant, you can find articles on how Jeff

Bezos made his ~~millions~~ billions, you can discover Bill Gates' secret to success, and Steve Jobs' personal philosophies.

Money-making knowledge abounds. On Wikipedia alone there's tons.

Here's where I have to do the thing where I tell you to ask your parents before looking online, blah, blah, blah, you know the drill. My legal team made me say that.

But seriously, the internet can be the unflushed toilet bowl of the human race. So stick to websites that don't tell you that you've just won a free laptop. Never give away your personal information, like your favorite flavor of ice cream. And try to not get distracted, no matter how interesting that article on Prince George looks. But you can learn a ton on the internet, so try it out.

Alternatively, you could check out your library for magazines like Entrepreneur, or Fast Company. Again, have your parents check those out, because sometimes they touch upon age-inappropriate things.

Devour Podcasts

Hello and welcome to another episode of Apps on Your iPhone That You've Never Used! Today we are going to be talking about the Podcasts app! You probably just said, "Huh? What's that?"

Well, it's basically radio on demand that is entertaining and/or educational. You can listen to podcasts in the car, while you are walking the dog, mowing the lawn...

Some podcasts teach you about making money, like EOFire, where John Lee Dumas interviews entrepreneurs who have made money, or How I Built This, a fantastic podcast by NPR which interviews wildly successful business people - like the founders of Crate & Barrel, 1-800-GOT-JUNK, Starbucks, and Ben and Jerry's, and asks them, "How did you build this amazing business?". Duh.

There are tons of others, but now I have to issue the same warning... Have your parents check the podcasts first to make sure they are "clean". Most of them are... but still.

On a side note, I have my own podcast for kids: The *Johncast*! It has everything a kid would like: jokes, prank calls, brutal roasts, special guests, and more!

Another side note, if your parents are reading this book and are interested in how to raise a *Kid Trillionaire* like myself (LOL), they might enjoy and benefit from my Dad's podcast - *The Einstein Blueprint.*

Find Interviews

When people make money and become famous, they often get interviewed on a variety of media. They may reveal their darkest secrets, like how they once ate a brussel sprout....and they liked it.

But they also share a ton of awesome tips and tricks, which can help bring you to the next level of money-making and entrepreneurship.

Interviews are so much better than school lectures, because these are real life stories and lessons from people who have been successful!

So go on the web, podcasts, wherever to find these interviews - also...

Mine YouTube For Money

YouTube is a goldmine! It hosts thousands upon thousands of videos that can help budding entrepreneurs like you make money.

Check out Caleb Maddix's channel and the Entrepreneur channel. Evan Carmichael has great interviews and content too. Watch TED Talks (have your parents watch them beforehand to make sure they are "clean"). Visit KidsGetRich.com for my latest YouTube channel recommendations!

While everyone else is watching cat videos and Minecraft on YT....you can instead watch Grant Cardone and Gary Vaynerchuk (profanity warning) and learn all about sales and motivation!

YouTube is chock-full of good content, but if the Internet is the toilet bowl of the human race, then YouTube is the spot with all the skid marks. Don't ever read the comments. Trust me on that one.

Take Practical Courses

There is this awesome website called Udemy. It has over 65,000 courses on anything you can imagine. For example, you could learn all about Photoshop, game design, coding, and even just making money in general. Most of them are cheap, or even free! Use the ratings get a sense of quality, and each course has "free" videos you can watch on a trial basis.

In addition to Udemy, there are many others:

- Lynda
- Skillshare
- Coursera
- Udacity
- Masterclass
- Adobe Creative Cloud Tutorials
- dPS (Digital Photography School, FREE!)
- Video Copilot (Video FX)
- So many others!

For example, I used Codecademy and Code School to learn how to code. One of my first jobs was making a website for a French café in London. I had learned how to code from those websites!

Codecademy was free, but it made me $60 when I was only 10 years old. Pretty awesome, huh?

Apprentice to a Master

You won't actually become an apprentice in the Colonial sense, because then you'd have to sign a 7-year contract. (LOL)

Like mentorship, this is one of the most time-efficient ways to learn about making money, but it's way more hands-on. Basically, what you do is find your rich business owner friend, relative, or neighbor and ask if you can work for them - even if you have to work for free.

My 14-year-old friend Mallory has had 3 different internships just in the past year. One at a bakery, her second at a juice shop, and her current one is at a bookstore.

Even if you're just getting coffee and running errands, you will still learn so much about whatever business it is by being what's called a "fly on the wall". You'll learn things firsthand that you can't possibly learn from a book or a podcast. Plus, you still might even get paid for your work! So get out there, find a master and beg to be their slave apprentice.

Peel Your Ears

Today, MJ DeMarco is rich; he made his money the new-fashioned way - with a website and selling online. But before that, he was a mere limo driver, where he had to wear a hat, say "Yes, sir..." as he opened the door for multi-millionaires.

He credits his later success to a single sentence he heard from some guy driving a Lamborghini, which happened to be MJ's dream car. MJ asked him what he did for a living, because the driver wasn't much older than him.

The young man said, "I'm an inventor."

MJ realized that you didn't need talent or luck to get rich. He then got off of his butt, and instead of continuing to trade his time for dollars, he created a website that would make him money every minute. MJ asked and listened, and he picked up that little gold nugget of advice. If you stop talking, open your mind, and listen, you'll see that there are *Trillionaire* ideas all within earshot.

Hang With Rich People

> *"You are the average of the five people you spend the most time with." - Jim Rohn*

If you hang out with people who are doing very well in life, then you will magically become like them. But if you are friends with losers, then you will become one, too, by default. Therefore, spend time with successful people!

My Dad is a member of a "mastermind group". And this is basically a bunch of entrepreneurs getting together regularly and helping each other out with their individual businesses. Now, you probably won't get to go to one now, but keep them in mind for the future!

However, you should definitely seek out other financially ambitious kids and befriend them. You can even join the entrepreneurship club at school, and if there isn't one, create your own! Do whatever you can to create your own network of *Kid Trillionaires*.

By the way, that quote by Jim Rohn above is true for all other areas of life, too. Are the people you hang out with bad influences? Or are they going to level you up to the lofty places where you want to go?

Go to Events

I regularly attend marketing conferences by a company called No B.S. Inner Circle. I've been to 10 so far in cities including Orlando, Phoenix, Cleveland, Chicago, San Antonio, and Atlanta. In fact, I've even spoken on stage at one!

Events provide a great opportunity to learn about any business or industry. They feature industry-leading speakers, vendors, and motivated attendees. They're like informal mastermind groups!

Let's say you sell candy in schools, and there is a candy trade show coming to your area. Yes, those actually exist. Get your parents to take you to it, and you might discover some new sugar bombs you can sell to your classmates. You might make a connection with a wholesaler!

Meet exhibitors, talk to as many people as possible, and you can even volunteer to help! I've done it before and once made $50 helping a vendor out at their booth! So going to events is a great way to generate business ideas, make connections, and jumpstart your *Trillionaire* quest.

Start Reading

> *"Read 500 pages every day. That's how knowledge works. It builds up like compound interest." - Warren Buffett*

Surprise, surprise there are actually books on how to make money! And a ton of them, too. Look, you're reading one right now!

You might hate to read, but understand that's only because school forces you to read boring books that seem to have no payoff. School math also seems infinitely boring, but once you add dollar signs to the numbers, and dollars to your pockets... Trust me, it might become the most fascinating subject in the world to you.

It's the same thing with books. Once you start making money with something you learned from a book, then books will become the most "funnest" thing in the world! The most successful people have been reading books not only to become rich, but to become even richer. We're going to go deeper into books and give you a list later on.

All I want you to know right now, is that you have to start reading to make money. And it's not just books. It's advertisements, newsletters, blogs, etc. Russell Brunson, the multi-millionaire founder of Clickfunnels, studied "junk mail" advertisements when he was 12. It's no wonder that he became who he is now.

Gain Valuable Experiences

> *"Only a fool learns from his own mistakes. The wise man learns from the mistakes of others." - various*

One of the best and fastest ways to learn about making money is actually to fail at making money. This might seem counterintuitive, but most rich people have built their fortunes on the lessons they've learned from multiple and often repeated failures.

Maybe you made a lemonade stand right next to a water fountain. Everybody went to the water fountain instead of your stand. What could you learn from this? Well, maybe to go to a location where people can't get water so easily next time - or sneakily unplug the water fountain!

But you don't have to just learn from your own mistakes, learn from other people's mistakes as well. So when you are studying other entrepreneurs through books, interviews, podcasts, whatever, pay close attention to the painful lessons they learned themselves. That will put you on a faster *Trillionaire* track.

Ready, Set, Go!

> *"Stop stopping!" - Russell Brunson*

I've just given you some super easy and mostly free ways to get started on your money-making quest. If you really want to get rich, you are going to have to become a student of wealth, entrepreneurship, and business.

Reading this book is a great first step and in this chapter I just gave you a whole bunch of powerful tips and ideas to get you going.

But honestly, it's still not enough. You are going to have to mentally get past your doubts, push through many obstacles, and overcome your own procrastination just to even get started.

CHAPTER 5

TRAIN YOUR BRAIN FOR GAIN

If you want to become rich, you're going to have to totally change the way you think about so many different things.

This may sound scary, but if you adopt this new and improved mindset, then it will be so much easier to make mounds of money.

Start Producing

Since the beginning of time, everyone used to weave their own clothes, grow their own food, and build their own house. But now, everyone buys all of these necessities, and produces almost nothing by themselves. All day long, they fork over their hard earned money to the producers. They are stuck on the losing side of almost every money transaction.

If you want to be a *Kid Trillionaire*, you need to switch over to the other side. Instead of thinking about how you can buy things all day long, you need to think about how you can sell things all day long. You need to transform yourself from a consumer to a producer!

For example, look at the iPhone. There's people who make the iPhones, and there's people who camp outside and wait in line for hours to buy the latest iPhone. Guess who's rich?

Start Helping

> *"A business that makes nothing but money is a poor business." - Henry Ford*

Most people, especially kids, only think about themselves. They walk around wondering, "What can I buy next?" and "What can I experience next?". They are very self-orbital.

But listen up. If you want to separate yourself from the crowd and become ultra-rich, you have to reprogram your brain so that you are always thinking about helping other people. If you look closely, you will see that every big company is fundamentally based on helping people.

Jeff Bezos started Amazon, which helps people buy what they need conveniently, at the click of a button.

Bill Gates started Windows, which helped millions upon millions of computer users save a lot of time and be much more productive!

If you really want to get rich, you have to understand that when you shovel your neighbor's driveway, you're actually helping them solve a problem, and that all business is about solving problems, helping others, improving lives, and even entertaining people! There's even a famous quote in the business world that goes something like this:

> *"If you want to make a billion dollars....try to help a billion people." - various*

Get Proactive

> *"It had long since come to my attention that people of accomplishment rarely sat back and let things happen to*

> *them. They went out and happened to things." - Leonardo da Vinci*

They say there are 3 types of people:

People who make things happen.

People who watch things happen.

And people who have no idea what the h*ck happened!

Obviously, the watchers and wonderers in the last two categories will probably never be rich.

Business is just like sports. If you stand still, with your hands in your pockets, picking your nose (quite a gymnastic feat!), you will never win or even score on the ballfield.

What will proactivity look like for you? You'll be setting goals, experimenting, and constantly creating opportunities for yourself.

Take Risks

> *"The biggest risk is not taking any risk....In a world that is changing really quickly, the only strategy that is guaranteed to fail is not taking risks." - Mark Zuckerberg*

From a very young age, you were probably taught that risk is a very bad thing. It's not your fault. Your parents, your teachers, everyone has been telling you, "Put on a bike helmet", "Don't run with scissors", "Get that fork away from the electrical socket". And the common sense stuff is solid advice, but in the business world, taking risks is rewarded.

In fact, you're never going to get rich unless you risk a little time, money, and reputation.

Most everyone else is deathly afraid of putting themselves out there. They're afraid of losing money, wasting their time, and having an embarrassing public failure.

Ordering a truckload of fidget spinners from China is risky. If nobody buys your spinners, then you just spent a ton of money on nothing. Knocking on doors to sell anything, also involves risk. The risk of rejection and feeling stupid.

But because everybody else is petrified of taking risks, that means there are massive advantages and huge opportunities for those few *Trillionaire* risk-takers!

Just remember, when you take a chance, use common sense. Always weigh the possible benefits versus the costs and the potential upside versus the downside!

Lose Limiting Beliefs

> *"Many people are passionate, but because of their limiting beliefs about who they are and what they can do, they never take any actions that could make their dream a reality." - Tony Robbins*

Limiting beliefs are ideas that you have in your head that tell you, "You can't do this." "You can't do that." "No, you're too young." "You're too stupid."

Limiting beliefs keep pretty much everybody who's poor from ever getting rich. There are tons of people in this world who would be rich if they weren't handcuffed by their own limiting beliefs.

Jeff Bezos left his comfy Wall Street job to create a website on this new thing called "the internet" where he could sell books. All his co-workers thought he was mad crazy - and even told him so directly. Obviously, if he had any self-doubts, we wouldn't have Amazon.com today, and he wouldn't be the richest guy in the world.

Richard Branson dropped out of school and started a record company. At any point, he might have said, "I can't do this! I'm a high school dropout!" If he did, he wouldn't be a multi-billionaire.

Tony Robbins' quote above is really accurate. Do you want to be yet another statistic and give up all of your dreams because of a stupid little thought in your head?

Hack Motivation

> *"When you feel like quitting, think about why you started."*
> *- internet*

Motivation is the fuel of your vessel on your *Kid Trillionaire* journey. It's what inspires you to keep going. It could be that fly Supreme hoodie you're saving up for. Maybe you want to impress all the kids at school.

Whatever it is for you, without it, you're not going to want to do the hard stuff, overcome obstacles, or really even try to make money. Thus, you won't become a *Kid Trillionaire.*

Maybe your parents are rich and they give you $2,000 a month for allowance. In that case, you might not be motivated to do anything at all. You're just going to sit in bed and play video games all day.

So in order to make money, you need to have sufficient motivation. And if you don't have enough, then when you try to make money, but you're not really into it, the second you run into an obstacle....well, let's say you have a lemonade stand, and nobody shows up. You're going to quit trying to make money, and you'll get discouraged. You need to be highly motivated. So how can you stay motivated?

Here are 3 hacks that I use. One is a reminder of what you are doing, for example while writing this book, I put a picture of the cover right by my desk, so every time I went to the computer I would see it.

The second one is something called an accountability partner. Basically, you remind each other about what you are working on. "Hey, I thought you were going to get that done." "How is ___ coming along?" An accountability partner can be anybody. It can be your parents, it could be your sister. You'll always be trying to impress them. "I finished that and did this!"

The final hack is to reward yourself. Make your first $100? Go buy yourself a treat! Or go to your parents and say, "Hey Mom and Dad, I worked really, really hard and made my first $100! Can we go out for ice cream?" And they will probably take you!

> *"People often say that motivation doesn't last. Well, neither does bathing - that's why we recommend it daily!" - Zig Ziglar*

Compete

> *"Business is the ultimate sport." - Mark Cuban*

The economy is super competitive. Companies are constantly fighting over customers, stealing ideas from each other, poaching the best employees from each other, and there's always downward pressure on prices and profits.

You might be making a killing selling contraband candy at your school, which recently removed all of the vending and soda machines. But someone else might see what you're doing, and start selling Snickers bars as well. And then your profits will tank.

> *"Work like there is someone working 24 hours a day to take it all away from you." - Mark Cuban*

No business is insulated from competition. You should always expect that someone is going to aggressively move in on your turf. A lot of times, they may even be unethical. Say your new competitor is the school bully, and he threatens to pummel you if you stay in business. I don't want to scare you, I just want to prepare you for the inevitable. You can always hire the bully two grade levels older to remind him who the candy kingpin really is! (Just kidding. Sort of. Maybe.)

One way to beat the competition is to totally change the game. Which babysitter would you hire? The plain old babysitter who plops the kids in front of a TV until bedtime, or the one who watches the kids, cleans the house, and teaches the kids how to read! Obviously the second one, because she differentiates her services! This is what my sister does. She says she will watch the kids and teach them to read.

Competition is actually great. It forces you to level up your game, deliver a great product at a great price, and also differentiate your business. On the flip side, competition also creates opportunities for you to move into other people's territory. Say it was the bully who was first selling candy. It would be well within your rights to sell M&Ms in the back of your classroom as well. Good luck.

Doesn't matter if you are a jock or a nerd, if you want to get rich, you're playing a high stakes game that can be highly competitive!

Ask and Thou Shall Receive

If you are a kid just starting out on your *Trillionaire* journey, you probably don't have a lot of capital in the bank and probably don't have a driver's license - never mind a car. You're going to have to ask your parents to drive you places. You might have to ask your parents to buy that first lawnmower and pay for your coding course so you can get your businesses up and running.

Also, no matter what you're selling, you're going to have to ask people to listen to you, to give you a chance, and ultimately for their money, all the time.

The simple act of asking is a powerful tool for making money, because it costs you nothing, and it can deliver infinite returns. For example, you could just ask people for feedback, ideas, or a referral, and you'd be surprised by how many people gladly accommodate. And you'll be surprised by how much it helps you grow your business!

There's even a very popular business book out titled *Ask*, by Ryan Levesque.

So whenever you're trying to making money, don't keep your mouth shut, don't be shy, just ask. You'll probably get a million no's. That's okay. Just keep asking.

It's even in the Bible, "Ask and thou shall receive." That's a useful principle to remember and apply, no matter what religion you believe in.

Embrace Change

Change is inevitable, especially in business. Nothing stays the same forever. It's a law of nature.

Now you might be excited because your fidget spinner business is going great and you are making a hundred bucks a month! You obviously don't want anything to change.

But all of a sudden, the party's over. The school bans fidget spinners because some bogus study said that it doesn't cure ADHD! So you might have to go outside your school to sell your fidget spinners, where it seems there's not as much opportunity. You might cry and wish you could sell in school again. You might get dejected and even close up shop.

But let's say you keep going, and you find this really rich kid who goes to a private school. He's trying to amass a bigger collection than everyone else, and he buys a ton weekly, and he tells all of his friends about you, and you make money from them. Now maybe you are making $200 a month. Now that's a better change.

Very rarely will change ever leave you completely without any new opportunities. Have you ever heard the expression, "Prepare for the worst and hope for the best."? That's what you should always do in business, and in life. Change isn't a bad thing. It's an awesome thing. There's always new and MASSIVE opportunities that come with change.

"Every exit leads to new entrances." - Chinese proverb

Think Accurately

This is the actually 11th principle from Napoleon Hill's ultra-famous book *Think and Grow Rich.* It basically means to make decisions using facts and logic.

Most people, who by the way aren't rich, do the opposite. They draw conclusions and take action based on personal opinions instead of hard evidence.

If you want to be successful and make lots of money in the business world, you can't afford reckless, inaccurate thinking. It will actually bankrupt you. You'll make terrible decisions, take on unnecessary risks, and lose money.

Say you're a weird fan of some new personality on YouTube. These days, it might be Logan Paul. His antics make you pee your pants laughing. So you come up with the brilliant idea to make and sell phone cases with the likeness of Logan Paul to your classmates. You spend $200 ordering these custom cases, confident that you're going to make a mint selling them, fast.

Only problem is, nobody in your class actually ever liked Logan Paul. It was just you. It turns out that not even the Dollar Store could sell your cases now. Heck, even the trash can closed its lid firmly shut as you were throwing them out!

Your mistake was not respecting the market's opinion. Had you known nobody liked Logan Paul, you wouldn't have lost $200.

If, instead, you had gauged demand before you ordered the cases, then you might not have lost any money at all. That would have been an example of accurate thinking that would have saved you a ton of money.

You have to make decisions using facts. You can't get emotionally attached to your ideas. In the business world, the customer is always right, and their opinions are the only ones that matter. If you don't listen to the marketplace, your business ventures will fail, and you'll get demoralized. Be honest with yourself, and always think clearly.

Stop Fearing Failure

In business, you will definitely fail many times over. But that's okay. You see, most entrepreneurs, on average, declare bankruptcy three times before they become successful. They bounced back from total failure, from losing all their money, multiple times!

So when you inevitably fail, definitely do not quit.

> *"Life is a cruel teacher. She loves to give you the test first and the lesson later." - Daymond John*

Learn from your mistakes, get back on your feet, and get back in the money-making game. You will never learn if you don't mess up. Failure isn't just an opportunity to improve, it's the only way to improve.

I have tried to make a lemonade stand many times, all of which have failed miserably.

From one of my most recent attempts, I learned that it's impossible to sell lemonade on a road where people are driving so fast they can't even see the sign. My uncle wasn't helping the marketing either. He was mowing the lawn in the front yard, wearing nothing but his underwear! I'm sure the sight of his bare chest and bikini briefs made the cars go even faster.

But one chilly October, I changed my approach a little, and sold pumpkins and hot chocolate. That was way more successful, because people were thinking, "Oh, I need a pumpkin for Halloween." Then they saw me, and I could solve their problem. I made so much money, I bought my uncle a pair of pants.

> *"I have not failed. I've just found 10,000 ways that won't work." - Thomas Edison*

So if you fail, shake it off and keep going. You are in good company. Failing is a natural part of making money.

Think Long-Term

Most kids only focus on their next test, their next holiday, and the very next whatever. They don't realize that now is a prime time to plant some money seeds that are going to pay off big-time in the long run.

The best example of not thinking long term is every teenager in America. Every 16-year-old wishes they had a car, but they don't have enough money for it because they blew all their money on video games and soda. So instead, they have to bum rides off of people, beg their parents, spend money on Ubers... it's pretty embarrassing.

> *"The best time to plant a tree was 20 years ago. The second best time is now." - Chinese proverb*

If you just look ahead a little bit and concentrate on your future a little bit....you will gain a MASSIVE head start on your *Trillionaire* journey. First of all, you won't waste every penny that comes your way on the latest fad.

Instead, you'll focus on how you can earn even more money. You'll save money, and, over time, create a fortune for yourself. You'll develop skills that will be useful in the future, like coding. You'll overcome small failures and mistakes.

But let's say you make a machine that makes any head of broccoli taste like candy and chocolate. There will always be a need for that, because everybody will want their broccoli to taste like chocolate, so that's not going to be a fad. In the long-term, long-term businesses will make more than short-term businesses. So think long-term to maximize your profits!

Believe In Yourself

If you're going to make money, you have to believe in yourself. This is going to sound really sappy but you really do, because if you don't think you can make money, then how will you ever make money?

> *"Whether you think you can or you think you can't, you're right." - Henry Ford*

He's basically saying if you believe you can do it then you can do it but if you don't believe it, you can't.

Everybody reading this book can make money, they can get rich. So believe in yourself. Don't tell yourself, "I'm a kid." "I'm a nerd." "I'm not strong." "I'm not smart." Don't tell yourself any of those things. Believe in yourself, because you can do it. You can get rich. All of you can get rich. So believe in yourself and get out there.

I definitely believe in you!

Think Outside The Box

By now, you've learned that one of the big, hidden secrets of making money is that you have to think differently. You have to throw out some of your existing thoughts and beliefs. And you definitely have to think differently than most of the people around you. To sum it up:

You have to think like a producer, not a consumer.

You have to think about helping others, not just yourself.

You have to think proactively, instead of passively.

You have to take risks, not avoid them.

You have to shed your limiting beliefs.

You have to motivate yourself, instead of just doing what adults tell you to do.

You have to be ready to compete.

You have to aggressively ask for the things you want.

You have to welcome and capitalize on change, not cry about it.

You have to think clearly and objectively.

You have to see failure as a necessary stepping-stone to success.

You have to look beyond the present and into the future.

Retrain your brain with all of these new mindsets, and you will be well on your way to becoming a *Kid Trillionaire.*

CHAPTER 6

SMASH THE MYTHS KEEPING YOU BROKE!

There are so many lies and false stories that can keep you from becoming rich. Let's debunk the biggest ones once and for all.

Rich People Are Lucky

One such myth is that all rich people are lucky. Sure, some of them are, e.g. lottery winners. But did you know that 70% of lottery winners go completely broke within 5 years?

But was Bill Gates really lucky? He spent over 10,000 hours teaching himself coding on a mainframe computer.

Or how about Donald Trump? He went bankrupt 7 times. Gosh, he doesn't sound very lucky.

Oprah Winfrey grew up with the misfortune of being dirt poor, but that didn't stop her from working hard and becoming a multi-billionaire.

You see, for the most part, rich people, as Gary Vaynerchuk says, "Worked their faces off!", to earn every single penny they got.

> *"I am a great believer in luck, and I find the harder I work, the more I have of it." - Thomas Jefferson*

So go ahead, shake off all of your bad breaks, learn from them, and make yourself some money!

Rich People Inherited Their Money

Another misconception is that rich people got all their money from their mom and dad.

Sure, some knuckleheads just had trust funds, yachts, and fancy cars handed to them on a Bitcoin-encrusted platinum platter. But if you focus on them instead of all the self-made multi-millionaires, you'll underestimate the power of your own hard work and miss out on all sorts of opportunities.

> *"I have consistently found that 80 to 86% (of millionaires) are self-made. That also applies to decamillionaires." - Thomas Stanley, the author of The Millionaire Next Door*

Howard Schultz, the founder of Starbucks, grew up in the housing projects of Brooklyn. Now he has almost $3 billion. He's a true rags-to-riches story.

You don't need to have rich parents to make money. Rich parents are a bonus, but are they required? Absolutely not.

In fact, one multi-millionaire, Daymond John, even says that poor kids have an advantage over rich kids when it comes to making money! The truth is, wealth is actually demotivational. These numbers below are really going to surprise you:

> *"Indeed, 70% of wealthy families lose their wealth by the second generation, and a stunning 90% by the third..." - Time Magazine*

You might not want to show your parents this section, because they might take away all your allowance. (LOL)

Rich People Are Evil

The biggest lie you will ever hear is that all rich people are evil.

And it's widespread, too. You may have noticed that in every movie, the rich guy is always a villain. You may remember Robin Hood, who steals from the rich and gives to the poor. Rich people have been unfairly demonized since the beginning of time.

It's just not true that rich people are inherently evil. Without them, we wouldn't have iPads, public libraries, modern medicine, or nearly the high standard of living that we enjoy today. Without rich people, there wouldn't be any opportunities or jobs for the rest of us!

If you buy into the myth that all wealthy people are evil, it will almost guarantee that you never get rich yourself....because who wants to be "evil"?

I Don't Have Good Grades!

> *"Grades don't measure anything other than your relevant obedience to a manager." - John Taylor Gatto*

A very common myth is that good grades in school will set you up for life. But if you do poorly in school, you will be doomed to a lifetime of failure and burger flipping.

You might think you won't ever be rich because you got a Z- on your last test, but that's just not true. Most millionaires and billionaires were C-students, flunkies, and dropouts. Grades and money have almost nothing to do with each other!

> *"I failed in some subjects….but my friend passed in all. Now he is an engineer in Microsoft and I am the owner of Microsoft." - Bill Gates*

Did you know that the comedian Jerry Seinfeld only got a B in acting? Now he's worth $900 million.

Winston Churchill got an F in English. He's considered one of the most articulate people of the 20th century.

Thomas Edison struggled mightily in school. If he was alive today, they probably would have put him on medication, and we might all still be reading by candlelight and whale oil.

William Rosenberg, the founder of Dunkin' Donuts, dropped out of school in 8th grade to support his family.

The smug Simon Cowell is another great example. He flunked out of school when he was 16 and now he's worth $500 million!

I'm not telling you to blow off school or your homework. Just don't let it give you false confidence or false discouragement about your prospects for becoming a *Kid Trillionaire.*

I Don't Have Time!

> *"Time is a created thing. To say 'I don't have time,' is like saying 'I don't want to'." - Lao Tzu*

You might think that you don't have any time to make money. After all, your schedule is filled up with schoolwork, sports, sleep, and video games.

But you don't actually have a time problem. You just haven't come up with enough powerful reasons to make money now. If you really want to do something, you'll figure out how to create the time for it.

It's right when your family goes out to the park, for a family picnic. You could be selling water to the other thirsty families there.

It's when you have a free period during school. You could be selling candy during that period instead of losing terribly at H-O-R-S-E.

You'll have school and summer vacations to make money. Even if you are at camp, you can run a side hustle there, too.

At my Boy Scout camp one summer, an entire troop bought all of the Mountain Dew Baja Blast from the trading post and resold them to other thirsty Scouts for double the price. What a bunch of jerks, right? But you have to respect how they made their money.

If you really want to get rich, you'll find the time. If not, then I'm surprised you made it this far into this book.

It's Too Hard!

> *"It is not supposed to be easy. Anyone who finds it easy is stupid." - Charlie Munger*

If you think becoming rich requires too much work and is not possible for you, then you have to at least realize that being broke is much, much harder.

You'll always worry about where your next dollar is coming from. You won't be able to buy anything. You'll be depressed. You won't have many friends. In other words, life is going to stink if you're broke. I have a whole chapter on the dark side later on...

> *"Nobody said it'd be easy. They just promised it would be worth it." - Anonymous*

I'm Too Shy!

> *"...I still have a shaky stomach before I go to a party, even before I sit down for dinner with close friends." - Steven Spielberg*

Maybe you aren't a people person. Maybe you get nervous at the mere thought of answering a question in class or saying "hello". Maybe, because of all of these things, you believe you won't ever be able to make serious money or run a business.

But that couldn't be farther from the truth.

For example, you can sell things online without showing your face, appearing on video, or even talking to anybody. Just look at how much stuff is being sold on Amazon. They were selling up to 600 items a second at its peak. I have a whole section later about how to sell things online.

Bill Gates was extremely shy when he was a kid. Now he's worth $91 BILLION.

Also, once you start down the *Kid Trillionaire* path, I guarantee that your self-confidence will skyrocket, and before you know it, you won't be as uncomfortable around people anymore.

So don't worry. You can still make money, even if you're shy!

By the way, that shy guy quoted above, Steven Spielberg, is worth $3.4 BILLION!

I'm Not Talented!

> *"Everything around you that you call life was made up by people that were no smarter than you." - Steve Jobs*

A very common myth is that all rich people are "talented" or "gifted" in one area or another. You might have been led to believe that you have to shoot hoops like LeBron James, act like Jennifer Lawrence, or sing like Justin Bieber to get filthy rich - because the only wealthy people you know are TV celebrities.

For example, Jeff Bezos isn't a sports superstar at all, and he is richer than any athlete or singer. Sure, having a beautiful voice can help. But when it comes to getting rich, there is zero talent required! Just a little bit of old-fashioned work.

There are actually people all around you who are quietly making money hand over fist in the business world. They may own real estate or have some weird company doing some rare thing that makes them a mint. These are the people you should aspire to become.

And remember, hard work beats talent every single time.

Plus, it's becoming increasingly clear that you actually don't even need talent in the music industry these days. Don't believe me? Just go listen to Justin Bieber or Jacob Sartorius.

Chasing Money is Unethical!

"Money is the root of all evil..." - popular myth

First of all, that's an oft repeated misconception. The Biblical quote is actually "The love of money is the root of all evil." As you can see, there's a big difference.

Too many people have an automatic negative association with money. Look around. You'll see that a lot of broke people have severe hang-ups and discomfort when it comes to money!

A lot of religious people think that chasing money is like worshipping a false god, and a lot of irreligious people are also very uncomfortable around money in general.

You might think that when you make money, your customers become poorer. That's called a zero-sum mindset....and it's 100% incorrect.

But remember, the essence of a profitable business is people helping other people.

In fact, if you have a great product or service that can really help people, and you sell it at a really great price, then it would be immoral to not provide it to others, and to not aggressively sell it!

I'm Poor!

> *"If you are born poor, it's not your mistake, but if you die poor, it is your mistake." - Bill Gates*

Most kids grow up thinking that they need money to make money. And lots of it, too. There's a popular narrative that only "the rich get richer."

Kids think, "I'm poor, therefore I can't make money." And so they don't even try, and it becomes a self-fulfilling prophecy.

There are plenty of ways to earn money even if you're flat-out broke. You could get a job. Duh! Almost no jobs require you to show up with a bucket of cash.

Build up your savings, and once you have a little money, then you can try to launch your own business, like selling candy in school.

Also, you could borrow money to start your business even though you couldn't scrape two nickels together on your own right now. After all, almost every business on Earth borrows money from banks and investors. I'm sure any adult in your life would be happy to lend you some money. You only need a very small amount to start out.

I'm an Immigrant!

> *"Give me your tired, your poor, your huddled masses yearning to breathe free..." - Statue of Liberty*

Uh, what does that have to do with anything? You could be from Mars and still make money. America actually became the wealthiest country on Earth because of the dreams and hard work of immigrants!

The founder of Yahoo!, Jerry Yang, came to America from Taipei when he was 8 years old. He only knew one word in English: shoe. Nevertheless, he went on to start Yahoo!, and his estimated net worth is $1.1 billion.

Indra Nooyi came from India and is now the CEO of PepsiCo, the second largest food and drink company in the world. Her salary is $20 million a year.

Sergey Brin was 6 years old when he left the U.S.S.R. with his family. He went on to start Google. He's worth $46 BILLION!

Need I go on? Don't let little things like where you came from stop you from making money. So make some money instead of making excuses!

I Don't Have a Perfect Idea!

> *"Don't spend so much time trying to choose the perfect opportunity that you miss the right opportunity." - Michael Dell*

News flash, you don't need a perfect idea. You don't even need a good idea. Even seemingly bad and stupid ideas can make you a ton of money.

For example...the Pet Rock. The guy who "invented" and marketed the Pet Rock became an overnight millionaire selling actual rocks. I am not even kidding. It was a rock in a box with googly eyes - check your grandparents' attic!

On late-night TV, you'll see ads for some of the most useless things that you didn't even know existed. Like the Wearable Towel. Or the Mermaid Snuggies. Best of all, the Cr*pTrap, which is a harness you put on your dog, and it has a little bag that catches the poop. Laziness to a whole new level.

The Snuggie has sold over $500 MILLION in revenue. It's a blanket you can wear like a sweatshirt!

So think of anything, no matter how stupid. I am not recommending selling something terrible and tricking people into buying it. Your product should still provide value and help people.

You see, if you sit around waiting for a perfect opportunity, you will miss out on tons of other opportunities. Don't use this myth as an excuse to procrastinate.

Nobody Will Hire Me!

> *"The biggest hurdle is rejection....be ready for it."* - *John Paul DeJoria*

You don't need to be hired to make money. In fact, you don't need to be accepted or said yes to instantly, either.

J.K. Rowling was rejected 10+ times before someone agreed to publish *Harry Potter*. Now Rowling is the world's richest author with over $650 million. Bet the other publishers were pulling their hair out.

Tim Ferriss was turned down by 25 publishers before one of them agreed to sell his book, *The Four-Hour Workweek*. He's sold 1.3 MILLION copies.

Jay-Z couldn't get anyone to release his first album. Now he has sold more than 36 million records. His net worth is $810 MILLION!

Harrison Ford, the actor who has played Indiana Jones, Han Solo, and many other iconic characters, was told, "You're never going to make it in the (acting) business, just forget about it." But Ford got the last laugh and quite a bit of applause over the years. He's now worth $230 million.

So don't let rejection keep you from making the money you are destined to earn.

I Don't Have Any Skills!

> *"You must either modify your dreams or magnify your skills." - Jim Rohn*

Don't think that because right now you can't code, promote yourself, invent things, knock on doors, etc. that you don't have the capabilities to make money. You can easily learn how to do all of those things!

Amazon's Jeff Bezos didn't know anything at all about the internet when he was a kid in 1975, because it didn't exist! Every expert was a beginner at some point.

For example, there's Udemy, Google, YouTube, Wikihow, books, all sorts of ways to learn these things. You have no excuses. We have already covered this in chapter 4.

You can cultivate useful skills working for someone else, through self-education, and through trial and error. Trust me, you'll grow *Kid Trillionaire* mad skillz!

For example, I'm learning how to make balloon animals, for free, on YouTube. Apparently, balloon sculptors can make $100-250 for a single birthday party! So don't worry about skills. You can acquire them super easily!

So there you have it. Those are all of the myths that will keep you from making money. Now that they're busted, go ahead and make some cash!

CHAPTER 7

BILLIONAIRES: WHERE DID THEY COME FROM?

Warren Buffett

> *"Rule no. 1: Never lose money. Rule no. 2: Never forget rule no. 1." - Warren Buffett*

When Warren Buffett was 6 years old in 1936, he bought a 6-pack of Coke for $.25, and sold the sodas for $.05 each. Do the math. He made a profit of $.05, which doesn't sound like much, but keep in mind it was a 20% profit.

At age 13, Warren sold newspapers in the neighborhood and also sold a horse-racing tip sheet because that's what they did in the 40s. As mentioned earlier, Buffett and a friend rented out a pinball machine to a barbershop. They ultimately did this multiple times, even selling the business to a veteran for a nice chunk of change.

Warren also tried various ventures, like selling gum, soda, peanuts, golf balls, and stamps. He had a short-lived car wash business. By the time he was 14 years old, Buffett had amassed $5,000. Keep in mind that was a long time ago. Today, in 2018, it would be like an 8th grader having $67,967 in the bank!

He wanted to skip college to focus on his many businesses, but his father overruled him. He tried to go to Harvard, but he got rejected. See? Billionaires had to overcome rejection and “no’s”, just like you and me!

At age 32, he finally became a millionaire after taking control of a business called Berkshire Hathaway. 55 years later, Buffett was worth over $80 BILLION.

So what’s the lesson here? That if you start grinding for coin early, you’ll set yourself up for a lifetime of MASSIVE success!

Michael Dell

> *“You don’t need to be a genius or a visionary, or even a college graduate for that matter, to be successful. You just need framework and a dream.” - Michael Dell*

When Michael Dell was a young child, he loved to make money. He washed dishes at Red Lobster, so he could pay for his stamp collection. He later sold the collection for $2,000!

In high school, Michael started selling newspaper subscriptions. He realized “cold-calling” wasn’t very effective, so he devised his own method, which was far more successful. He targeted couples who just got married or just got a home, who were much more likely to buy. In a single year, he earned $18,000, which was more than his economics teacher at the time.

When Dell was 15, he bought his first computer. He quickly disassembled it to see how it worked.

In college, Dell started a computer company and soon it would become one of the top companies in the world! You may know it. In fact, I’m typing on a Dell computer as I write this.

Now Michael didn’t just work hard, he worked smart as well. Who would have thought to use a different method for selling people subscriptions? So don't just work hard when it comes to making money. Use your brain too!

Elon Musk

> *"I think it is possible for ordinary people to choose to be extraordinary." - Elon Musk*

Do you think the bullies in your school are bad? Well, listen to what Elon Musk had to go through:

"They got my best friend to lure me out of hiding so they could beat me up. And that hurt. For some reason they decided that I was it, and they were going to go after me nonstop. That's what made growing up difficult. For a number of years there was no respite. You get chased around by gangs at school who tried to beat the $#!^ out of me, and then I'd come home, and it would just be awful there as well."

This was all when Musk just around 13 years old, living in South Africa.

They probably picked on him because he loved to read. He would read upwards of 10 hours a day! He read the entire Encyclopedia Britannica by age 9. Elon credits most of his success with Tesla and SpaceX to having read lots of science fiction as a kid.

Musk also loved to tinker with electronics. He learned how to code on a computer and made a simple game called Blastar, in the style of Space Invaders. He even sold the code for it to a computer magazine for $500.

When Elon was 19, he attended the University of Pennsylvania, which is actually where my Dad went at the exact same time. Instead of just renting a room to live in, Elon rented an entire ten-room house and basically turned it into party central. He charged his classmates $5 for entry and cheap beer….and made a mint before he even graduated.

Right out of college, Musk started a company called Zip2, and four years later, made a personal profit of $22 MILLION!

Believe it or not, Elon actually thanks his bullies from his childhood. He says that everyone needs adversity to become truly successful. So learn from Elon. He started early. He read books. He was messing around with technology. He took advantage of the fact that kids in college love to party and made tons of money.

Bill Gates

"Patience is a key element of success." - Bill Gates

When Bill Gates was a kid, he was obsessed with business books and had read a bunch long before high school, long before he ever touched a computer.

In 9th grade, his parents sent him to a private school where he met his new best friend, Paul Allen. They would spend hours upon hours in the computer lab.

Bill even got kicked out of the lab for exploiting the computer systems to get extra time on them. He got his privileges back when he debugged the program (that he messed up). Soon enough, Bill was in charge of the scheduling program for the school. He then used his position to place himself in a class with a "disproportionate amount of interesting girls".

When Bill was 15, he and Paul made a computer program called "Traf-o-Data", and earned $20,000 selling it to another company.

Bill went to college in Boston and Paul went to college in Seattle, but these friends still stayed in touch. Soon they both dropped and started a computer company called Microsoft. You might have heard of it! It became successful incredibly fast, and now, 37 years later, Bill Gates is one of the world's richest people, with over $90 BILLION as I am writing this.

So the lesson here is to take full advantage the resources you have right in front of you. Bill had access to computers, he not only learned how to use them but learned how to create software that would help an enormous amount of people - remember he had learned all about business when he was in middle school.

Richard Branson

> *"You don't learn to walk by following the rules. You learn by doing and by falling over." - Richard Branson*

Richard Branson struggled mightily in school. He may have even had something called dyslexia. He bounced from one school to another, getting in trouble at pretty much all of them. One of his principals predicted that he would either become a criminal or a millionaire. Eventually, he dropped out of high school altogether.

Despite his horrible school experience, he actually started a magazine for high schoolers called *Student*. It was a massive hit, and Richard used the money he made from it to start a mail-order record company called Virgin Records.

This probably makes zero sense to you, so let me explain. If someone wanted to listen to music back in the 70s, they would use this big, bulky thing called a record player. And instead of downloading music onto the record player, they would put in this thing like a really big DVD. And then the record player would play the DVD. Pretty weird, huh? Why didn't they just download the music from Spotify and play it on their iPhone X? Oh yeah, they didn't have those.

So basically, Richard's company was like Amazon for records. And he made enough money off of it to open a physical record store and recording studio. All of a sudden, famous bands like the Rolling Stones and Genesis would record with Virgin Studios. Virgin would go on to become one of the top six record companies in the world. And this was all while Richard was still in his early 20s.

Branson continued on to create Virgin Atlantic airlines, Virgin Megastores, Virgin Train, and he is even trying to start a space-tourism company, Virgin Galactic! Now, Richard is worth $5.2 BILLION! Pretty good for someone whose principal gave a 50/50 chance of becoming a criminal.

So maybe you struggle in school. Maybe you can't read and ~~rite~~ write as well as everyone else. That's okay. Richard has proved that you can still make mountains of money! Richard also taught us that we should use one success as a foundation for another.

Sara Blakely

> *"Failure is not the outcome - failure is not trying. Don't be afraid to fail." - Sara Blakely*

Sara was just 7 years old when she started her own business: sewing little charms onto white socks and selling them to her classmates.

Later, as a teen, Sara created a beachside babysitting business. Parents would pay her to make sure their toddler didn't get eaten by a shark while they were sunbathing. She tried to expand her business to nearby hotels, but received a very sharp "No!". She says that this was an important lesson that rejection and failure aren't bad things. Her father would ask her regularly what she failed at. If she didn't fail at anything, then she wasn't trying anything new.

When Sara was 16, her father gave her a couple of motivational recordings titled "How to Be a No-Limit Person" by Dr. Wayne Dyer. Sara credits these tapes for her future success. She listened to them so many times, she had them memorized!

Later, Sara had a bunch of odd jobs, like working at Disney, and selling fax machines. A fax machine is what they used before they had email. It was a big thing because you could send a letter over the phone lines obviously without a stamp with it. No, I'm not explaining what a letter and a stamp is...

But while Sara was selling these relics from the past, she had an idea for a new business. She went on to start a company called Spanx, which basically sold tights without the feet, and jazzed it up a bit by saying that wearing them made you look thinner. It was a smash hit and Spanx even got on the list of

Oprah's Favorite Things! Now Sarah owns 100% of the company and is worth over a billion dollars!

Sara gave us several great lessons. Start early. Accept failure. We talked about this two chapters ago. Learn as much as you can about motivation and making money. Finally, don't ever give up part of your company unless you absolutely have to. Sarah would be worth a lot less if she had taken on partners or investors along the way.

Thomas Edison

"There is no substitute for hard work." - Thomas Edison

Thomas Edison attended public school for about 3 months before his mother pulled him out. He was just 12 years old when he convinced his parents to let him sell newspapers on the train. He even made his own newspaper, the Grand Trunk Herald, which was very popular with passengers.

While working on the train, little Thomas used to perform chemical experiments in the baggage car. One day, he accidentally set the car on fire. Whoops! He quickly got kicked off of the train and had to sell the newspapers at the stations instead.

When Edison saved a 3-year-old from getting hit by a train, the tyke's grateful father taught Edison how to use a telegraph. A telegraph was something they used before they had a telephone. A telephone is what they used before they had cell phones. Cell phones are what they used before they had iPhones. Telegraphs are really, really old. After all, this was 1862.

When Edison was 15, he had learned enough to become a telegraph operator. He did this for many years until his partial-deafness forced him to quit.

Edison moved to Boston where he designed an electronic voting recorder. But the Massachusetts lawmakers didn't want to use it. Dejected, he went to New York City and invented an improved stock ticker. A stock ticker is what they used to read the prices of the stocks - like a scrolling headline on the

TV. This invention was a success, and the Gold and Stock Telegraph company was so impressed, they paid him $40,000 for it!

You probably know the rest. His inventions changed the world. Edison went on to invent the light bulb, the phonograph, and many other amazing inventions. Ultimately he owned about 1,000 patents. Edison got rich and was worth the equivalent of $217 million in today's currency.

What's the lesson here? Inventing stuff can make you some serious coin! Oh, and start working early too.

Andrew Carnegie

> *"No man can become rich without himself enriching others."*
> *- Andrew Carnegie*

Andrew Carnegie moved from Scotland to America when he was 13 years old in 1848.

His first job was in a cotton factory where he made a measly $1.20 per week.

Soon, Carnegie got a better job as a telegraph messenger, just like Thomas Edison. He was quickly promoted to an operator for his outstanding work.

He sensed that railroads had more opportunity than telegraphs, so he took a job as the assistant to Thomas Scott, a top official in the railroad system.

Andrew learned everything about railroads and business through this job. After working hard and making connections, he was promoted and given tons of responsibility.

While working for the railroads, Andrew made many smart investments that turned out to be very successful. One day, he saw what steel could do, and how it's superior to iron, and decided that it was going to be the future. He quit the railroads and started Carnegie Steel Company.

Steel grew in high demand, and Carnegie was incredibly successful. Carnegie was even one of the richest men in history, with over $300 BILLION at his death! That's way more than even Jeff Bezos, the founder of Amazon.

Andrew Carnegie taught us many valuable lessons. You can still be successful, even if you are an immigrant. You always have to stay on the cutting edge. Steel was the next big thing, and Carnegie saw it coming, left his comfy place in the railroad industry, and took full advantage of the opportunity.

John Rockefeller

> *"Don't be afraid to give up the good to go for the great." - John Rockefeller*

John Rockefeller was 16 years old when he tried to get a job. He went everywhere in Cleveland, only to be rejected each time. So he went around again. He even asked the same place 3 times before he was given a job as a bookkeeper. He kept records of sales, transactions, and expenses. He worked very long and tedious hours, but did his job very well and got promoted.

It's also worth noting that John's father was a con artist, who tried to "cheat my boys every chance I get", hoping it would "make them sharp". And I think it's bad when my Dad won't give me the $50+ he owes me!

John went on to start a business with his neighbor Maurice. They became "commission merchants" and sold groceries. Together, they made $40,000 in one year, which is not bad for a 22-year old! Then the Civil War happened. Did I not mention this was 1863? (LOL) This made the price of grain and corn go way up, and the partners made even more money.

Later in life, John made a fortune selling oil. Keep in mind that not many people drove cars back then. But driving started to become more and more commonplace, so gasoline would soon be in very high demand. John ended up worth $192 BILLION, by some estimates.

John was very persistent. Persistent means to keep at it, to have a lot of grit.

He asked every single shop in Cleveland if he could get a job multiple times! So just keep going, keep trying, and you could be the next Rockefeller.

Daymond John

> *"If people haven't laughed at your dreams, then you aren't dreaming big enough, just keep pushing forward." - Daymond John*

Daymond started hustling for dough when he was only six. He sold customized pencils to the prettiest girls in school. But his principal quickly put a stop to it when he discovered that Daymond was stealing the pencils from kids he didn't like. (LOL)

When Daymond was 10, his parents divorced and he lived with his mom. All of a sudden, he was poor. He tried to help by handing out flyers for $2 an hour.

Since Daymond was dyslexic, like Richard Branson, he barely graduated high school. He waited tables at Red Lobster to make a little cash. One day his mom asked him what he wanted to do with his life. And Daymond said he wanted to make clothes for young men, so she taught him how to make wool caps. He made 80 caps with cheap fabric and sold them for $10 apiece, grossing $800.

When interviewed on a podcast, he was asked if he made more caps the next day. Daymond replied, "No. I went back the next hour and sewed more."

Daymond's mom mortgaged her house to help his new clothing business, called FUBU. FUBU was even featured in many popular music videos, but Daymond amazingly still worked at Red Lobster!

After 2 years, Daymond finally quit his job and focused on FUBU full-time. His company went on to sell $6 BILLION worth of clothes! When FUBU became less popular in the early 2000s, Daymond became an even bigger celebrity by starring in the famous TV show Shark Tank.

Daymond overcame childhood poverty, having no father, no education, and dyslexia. He's now worth over $200 MILLION! What's your excuse again?

Ben Franklin

> *"An investment in knowledge pays the best interest." - Ben Franklin*

Ben Franklin's formal education ended when he was 10, because his parents could not afford school. He was then apprenticed to his brother James, a printer. An apprenticeship means that you have to work for this person for a certain amount of years, usually more than 4 - it is a form of semi-slavery, really. On the plus side, Ben learned everything about the printing press, which is not found at Staples anymore.

When Ben was 15, his brother started one of the first independent newspapers in America, *The New-England Courant.* Ben really wanted to write in the newspaper, but was denied the chance. Instead, he sent letters under the fake name of Mrs. Silence Dogood, pretending to be a middle-aged widow. The letters became very popular and were discussed all over the city.

Ben was a supporter of free speech, and when his brother was jailed for publishing articles that the governor didn't like, Ben took over the newspaper, and published another letter from Mrs. Dogood, saying, "Without freedom of thought there can be no such thing as wisdom and no such thing as public liberty without freedom of speech." Benjamin swiftly ran away from his uncompleted apprenticeship.

He moved to Philadelphia, hoping to make a fresh start. Ben was technically a fugitive, because he didn't complete his apprenticeship. There he jumped around from one printing job to another before eventually starting his own newspaper and printing shop. He published *The Pennsylvania Gazette* even though he was just 17 years old! Surprisingly, Ben actually made lots of money right away.

After achieving much success with his newspaper, he wrote *Poor Richard's Almanac*, which was also a smash hit for decades. You have to understand that newspapers were like the social media of the time. So Ben's newspaper was like Facebook crushing all of the competition today.

He used his newfound power and influence to become the first Postmaster of the United States. Not only was he crushing his industry rivals, he also took control of the postal service. Now he could deliver his newspapers faster than his competitors.

Ben earned over $43 million (in today's currency), but he accomplished way more than just that. He moved to London and back, started a library and a scholar's association, tried to run for political office, invented the gas oven, founded the University of Pennsylvania, created the first fire department in Philadelphia, researched electricity (those kites with the keys!), and was one of the Founding Fathers of the United States of America!

Ben taught us would-be *Kid Trillionaires* so, so many lessons about how to overcome and succeed.

Ingvar Kamprad

> *"Only those who are asleep make no mistakes." - Ingvar Kamprad*

When Ingvar was just 5 years old, he sold matches in his little Swedish town. Not the highest paying gig, but then again he was only 5. When he was 7, he started using his bicycle to sell matches to his neighbors farther away. He was buying the matches dirt cheap from Stockholm and selling them for an amazing profit. He expanded to sell fish, Christmas tree decorations, seeds, and pens and pencils.

When Ingvar was 17, he started selling replicas of his uncle's kitchen table. It became a mail-order business, where people would send him money and he would ship them a table.

Ingvar started to sell other furniture, too. His business just became more and more popular and finally morphed into the furniture mega-giant it is today called IKEA.

I am even writing on an IKEA table right now! So Ingvar went from selling matches and fish to founding a $13 BILLION company!

He started his empire when he was in kindergarten! Why again haven't you started yet?

Sean Parker

> *"A million dollars isn't cool. You know what's cool? A billion dollars." - Sean Parker*

When Sean Parker was 7 years old, he learned how to program computers. When he was 15, he got caught hacking into a very successful company by the FBI and was sentenced to community service. That escalated quickly!

Sean went on to intern for many companies, remarkably earning $80,000 while still in high school. He and a friend started a website called Napster, which let people share their music files with each other - sort of illegally. It was an instant success, but it couldn't last.

It ended disastrously when Sean got fired from his own company, and the recording companies sued Napster for $1 TRILLION! I am not even joking! If he lost, he could have been the first Negative *Kid Trillionaire.*

Sean was going to keep trying, though. He founded Plaxo, which was pretty much an online address book. But Sean got fired from his own company, again! It's sort of like taking care of a dog, feeding it, taking it out on walks, picking up its poop, and then having it bite you.

Dejected, Sean looked into this new thing called social media. When he was 24, he met Mark Zuckerberg, they hit it off, and he became the first president of Facebook. Now Sean is a multi-billionaire. I guess the third time's the charm!

Sean failed and failed... but he kept going. Eventually, he hit a grand slam home run.

More Great Examples

J.K. Rowling wrote her first book when she was 6. It was about a rabbit who had measles.

Carlos Slim, a Mexican billionaire, started learning about business at a very young age.

When Brian Scudamore, the founder of 1-800-GOT-JUNK was a kid... he saw his neighbor start a car wash business... and this future businessman also started a car wash, but for $.50 cheaper!

Amancio Ortega, the founder of several clothing stores such as Zara, learned how to make clothes by hand at 14.

Mark Zuckerberg made an IM system for his family when he was 14. He later went on to start Facebook, duh.

Chinese billionaire Li Ka-Shing had to drop out of school when he was 15 and go work to support his family. Hey, I just realized. Ka-Shing = Cha Ching! ILLUMINATI CONFIRMED!

Cornelius Vanderbilt quit school at 11 and started working. At 16, he had his own ferry business in NYC. He made eventually made billions in the shipping and railroads industries.

The One BIG Lesson

See how all of these rich people worked when they were young? If you only take away one thing from this book, it's to start early. Like NOW.

CHAPTER 8

LEMONADE STAND 2.0

There are so many ways to make money, it's insane. But not all methods are equal. For example, selling hot chocolate in the Sahara Desert is not a great idea. So here are some of the best things a kid can do to make money.

Beyond The Lemonade Stand

Every kid has tried a lemonade stand, or some variation of one. Me and my sister had a very successful baked goods stand. But by itself, a lemonade stand probably can't make more than $100 in a single day. It depends on the weather for one thing....plus it's hard, long work - and if your parents ever charge you for the ingredients, it might become an even bigger waste of time. Thankfully, there are far better ways to become a *Kid Trillionaire* than selling lemonade.

Affiliate

Affiliate marketing is a fantastic way to make money. You get paid a commission for selling somebody else's products. What's great about this is that you don't have to invent anything new, you don't have to buy inventory, and the only thing you are risking is your time! Plus, the better the product, the easier it is for you to sell.

You can even sell online these days. You can have a page where you review toys and give a special affiliate link to Amazon - like that millionaire kid from EvanTube. So how can you become an affiliate?

There is something called Amazon Affiliates, and if you sign up for it, you can make links for anything on Amazon. And you can put these links in your YouTube videos, your Instagram posts, your Tumblr (just kidding), your email signature, anything! Whenever someone clicks the link and buys anything on Amazon, you get money! So they might go and buy the toy you advertised, and then buy a TV for a couple thousand bucks, and you get a percent of all of it.

Almost major sites like Amazon also have affiliate programs. You can also work out your own system with someone else. Affiliate marketing is way better than a lemonade stand because you can make a lot more money selling as an affiliate than you can by selling yellow sugar water. Kids have already made millions doing this. Why can't you?

Code For Cash

> *"Coding is the foreign language of the future." - internet meme*

In this day and age, everything is either on your phone, tablet, or computer. That's why knowing how to code is a great skill. But I'm not talking about making games on Khan Academy. I'm talking about building websites. My uncle's company paid another company $3,000+ for a website! (The funny part is, I would have done it for $200!) But imagine getting $3,000 just for typing some lines of code!

The good news is, every single school, big company, etc. is trying to teach kids how to code. But none of them is teaching kids how to make money with it. I remember the first time I made a website for someone and got paid. It was only $60, but to 10-year-old me, it was a fortune. If you want to see the whole story, sign up for more content at KidsGetRich.com!

I would recommend Codecademy, or Code School if your parents would get it for you. I wouldn't recommend learning Python, even though it is super popular at the moment. Instead, learn Javascript, HTML, and CSS. Those actually are used in making websites. Python is for babies who can't tie their own shoes! Only idiots who think the name sounds cool actually use it!

On the other end of the spectrum, making apps and games for iPhones can actually make you a fortune. You make the next Angry Birds and you will be loaded for life. Remember Thomas Suarez, the creator of Bustin Jieber? He made lots of money, so can you.

Finally, old people are pros at getting viruses on their computers. They often can't figure out how to get rid of them. So if you know how to get rid of viruses, then you could make a killing!

Coding is better than a lemonade stand because you can simply make so much more money.

Peddle Pure Sugar

> *"Math Problem: John has 32 candy bars. He eats 28. What does he have now?...Answer: Diabetes" - internet*

No, I don't mean sugar cane. I'm talking about the stuff that kids obsess over all day long. Cookies, candy, soda, those sort of inorganic things.

You see, there is an inexhaustible demand for junk food by kids in school, or really anywhere. They could eat 5 Snickers bars, be just about to throw up, and they'd still be figuring out how they can get their hands on a 6th.

And your school might have gone straight-up Nazi and removed all vending machines, which is even better for you. The only high-fructose corn syrup will be in your backpack, for sale – at premium prices!

These are the absolute ideal selling conditions. Listen to copywriting legend Gary Halbert:

> *In any case, after my students are finished telling me what advantages they would most like to have, I usually say to them something like this: "O.K., I'll give you every single advantage you have asked for. I, myself, only want one advantage and, if you will give it to me, I will (when it comes to selling burgers) whip the pants off all of you!"*
>
> *"What advantage do you want?" they ask.*
>
> *"The only advantage I want," I reply...*
>
> *"Is... a STARVING crowd!"*

If you sell Twix bars, brownies, and Red Bull in school, you will most definitely make boatloads of money. After all, nobody eating terrible cafeteria food is going to say, “Can someone PLEASE get me a celery stick? I’ll pay five dollars.” But they will pay that, if not more, for a sugary relief from the pain of school and the Ezekiel bread-avocado sandwich mom packed them.

Just listen to this British boy bragging:

“No one has done what I have. Others have sold sweets, I’ve created an empire.”

He thinks he’s the Pablo Escobar of “sweets”. But who could blame him for getting a swelled head? He was making $1,400 a week and about $70,000 a year before the school system shut him down!

So how do you deal Snickers out of the back of the classroom?

First you buy the goods - and get the sugar as cheaply as possible. Check out wholesale stores like BJ’s. Stick to the classics and get Snickers, M&Ms, Milky Ways, etc. Don’t get stuff nobody likes. *cough cough* Barfies. *cough cough*.

Then you figure out the prices. It's pretty easy to do this. If you bought a pack of 20 Snickers for $10, then each bar cost you $.50. Obviously, you want to make money, so sell each bar for $.75 to $1 or even more depending on how rich your classmates are.

But to attract more customers, make deals, like 3 bars for $2.50...You might think that isn't much, but when 100+ hungry, sugar-addicted boys and girls are throwing money in your face, you'll change your mind.

All you have to do now, is sell. Try to sell before lunchtime, when kids will be hungrier and will buy more. And try not to get caught. But chances are that you won't. Worst comes to worst, have a fall guy ready. This could be your mean older brother. Tell them that he made you do it and he takes most of the money. Give him some money so he plays along. Chances are you won't get in trouble.

Another British kid (Tommie Rose) earned $22,000 before he got caught. That's way more than the neighborhood rich kid's allowance. I don't know what he's doing now, but I don't think he'd let the schools stop him from getting rich.

You don't have to just sell at schools. You can sell sugar anywhere there are kids, like summer camp, playgrounds, festivals, anywhere! I have a friend who sold candy at his brother's wrestling matches.

Selling junk food is a much better way to make money than a lemonade stand because you simply have a much larger market and greater demand.

Mind Creatures

> *"A baby-sitter: a teenager acting like an adult while the adults are out acting like teenagers." - the internet*

Babysitting is a simple way for kids to make money. Older kids have been doing it since the age of the dinosaurs. Remember your babysitter? They probably plopped you in front of the TV and stared at their phone the whole time. If you babysit, you could watch a movie with the kids or do your homework....and get paid for it!

Yeah, if you had wild brats who pooped their diaper every two seconds, babysitting could be hard. I recommend waiting a little before you change their diapers – ya know, make sure they are done! And if you aren't quite old enough to babysit, you could become a mother's helper instead - sort like an apprenticeship.

Petsitting is generally far easier. My sister would petsit this cute little dog called Ella that would just sit in my sister's lap practically the whole time. And Christine got paid $10! That might not seem like much, but my sister just did nothing and got paid - and she was only 11! And remember, you don't have to petsit big dogs who are going to take giant turds, or that cat you are afraid of. You can choose whom you work for.

Baby/petsitting is better than a lemonade stand because it's actually a fun way to make money. If you like working with children younger than you, or you want to take care of a fuzzy little dog, then this is the gig for you.

Sell Scrap

"One man's trash is another man's treasure." - idiom

Last summer, my Dad put a massive, old, rusty, broken air conditioner out on the curb. Some random person actually hauled it away, and my Dad couldn't imagine why.

Later, my father put out a second broken air conditioner. It, too, disappeared in an instant. Then he put out a third air conditioner, because we were moving to a tiny apartment in NYC and needed to get rid of almost all of our stuff. Somebody took that one too! A month later, my Dad's friend told him that the town dump pays $20 for air conditioners in any form. Who knew? I guess whoever scooped them up knew. So my Dad could have taken them to the dump and made $60 himself.

Another time, we were cleaning out our house, and we had these big dumpsters that we were filling up with all sorts of junk. And this guy knocked on the door and asked if he could go through the dumpster. My Dad let him. He was probably looking for scrap metal, like copper and aluminum. Metals have become so valuable, that scrappy people are going through junkyards and old machines and harvesting them for profit. That's what this guy was doing.

When Cameron Herold was 7 years old, he would go door-to-door and asked people if they had any wire coat hangers. Cameron would then sell the hangers for 3.5¢ to dry cleaners. He would eventually become a highly successful entrepreneur and the COO at 1-800-GOT-JUNK.

Joel Holland, the founder of VideoBlocks, retrieved lost golf balls from the woods at the golf course when he was 8. He then sold them right back to probably the same people who lost them!

A lot of "junk" can actually be worth good money. So next time your parents are throwing out a washing machine, just check and see if you can mine some copper or aluminum. There's really no risk to selling junk because it's freely available. Selling scrap is better than a lemonade stand because it has 100% profit margin, and you don't need the weather to be warm and sunny!

Open a Bank

> *"I rob banks because that's where the money is." - Willie Sutton, Bank Robber*

So let me tell you about this 19-year-old kid at my Dad's work. He would walk around saying, "$20 raffle! $20 raffle!" People who wanted to enter would write their name on a $20 bill, fold it up, and put it in a hat. Once twenty people had entered, he would take the hat and pull a random bill out of it. Whoever's name it was on the bill would win all $400 (really $380, right?).

So what does this have to do with making money? Well, whoever won would usually tip the kid who ran the raffle around $20-$50. So this kid just made some easy money without taking on any risk. He just took his cut of a big pool of money. This is really what banks and Wall Streeters do. They get a whole bunch of money together, and they take a percentage for themselves. The bigger the pool of money, the bigger their cut.

You could do this too! You could run a raffle at school, in your local neighborhood... A lot of kids have been running football pools and NCAA basketball pools and making lots of money for a very long time!

I'm not condoning gambling, nor am I condemning it, one way or the other. I just want you to understand that the world of banking is filled with money-making opportunities. For example, when you're out with your brother and he doesn't have any money for the ice cream cone he's dying to get, you could lend him $5 with the condition that he has to pay you $7 once you get home! Do that all day long and in larger quantities, and you'll have more money than Buffett! People may start calling you Shylock but whatever...

Finance is way better than selling lemonade, because just look who has more money, kids at lemonade stands, or Wall Street suits?

Social Media Riches

> *"They say social media is a unicorn, but maybe it's just a horse." - internet*

Everyone, both kids and adults, are wasting most of their lives on social media. Instead of joining them, you can use their addiction to make money. For example, kids have made thousands of dollars selling custom filters on Snapchat since that feature came out a few years ago.

Kids have also made serious bank on YouTube in a variety of ways for years. We've talked about EvanTube, but there are many, many, many others. Like Michelle Phan, who made millions by publishing simple makeup tutorials for 10 years. Justin Bieber and his musical talents(?) were "discovered" on YouTube. Now he's worth $225 million. Instead of just watching YouTube videos, he made them.

Let's face it, most older people can't figure out how to use social media. Your aunt might have a business, and needs a social media page. But she doesn't want to make it, and quite frankly, she doesn't know how. You can create and manage it for her in exchange for some money.

Lastly, the founders of all these successful social media networks all were young. Mark Zuckerberg, David Karp (mentioned earlier), and Chad Hurley, founder of YouTube, were all about 25 years old when they created their network. They are all incredibly freakin' rich.

Ride Trends

"The trend is your friend…" - Wall Street trading motto

If you can spot the next big fad coming to your school or your neighborhood, then you can easily make a ton of money on it.

You already know this. Just think how much money you could've made with fidget spinners in 2017 if instead of buying one or two, you bought a hundred early on and sold them to other kids. What if you had the foresight to buy 3,000 of them at a low price and sell them as the price skyrocketed?

I heard someone ordered 1 MILLION spinners for $2 each from China and sold them all for a massive profit before they even got off the boat!

And the opportunity to make bank wasn't just in regular spinners. It was in fidget cubes, those chrome spinners, the light-up ones, the gear variants, etc.

By the way, the fidget spinners were popularized by these two 17-year-old kids with a 3D printer. They made $350,000 in the first six months of selling them!

And what about slime? That was another big fad. Kids in my town were selling gobs of slime to each other. Some of the buyers don't know how to make it themselves, or were banned from making it at home by their parents! But they just have to have it, because they don't want to be the only kid without slime. One girl made $3,000 a month selling slime on Instagram.

Do you remember Crocs? Well, a couple became millionaires after creating Jibbitz, those little charms you put on Crocs. (Kids, please don't let your parents wear Crocs!)

Right now, where I live in New York, there is this massive mania where people are buying everything they can from this company called Supreme. Savvy kids are literally making thousands of dollars reselling Supreme apparel to their rich classmates all over the world.

The creator of Loom Bands was worth over $100 million. Two women trying to make money off of the trend sold a dress made out of Loom Bands for $234,000! Unfortunately for them, the person they sold it to took the dress and refused to pay them their money... So always be aware of scammers and thieves.

My point is, there will always be crazy new trends and fads. If you can capitalize on them, you will become a *Kid Trillionaire*. So when you see the next big thing coming, remember the lesson of the fidget spinner - and figure out how you can sell the next big thing instead of figuring out how you can buy it, like everyone else.

Do I even have to say how much more opportunity there is here than in a lemonade stand?

Tutor

> *"Dear math, stop asking me to find your x. He's not coming back." - meme*

If you've made it this far into this book, then clearly you are an ambitious, really smart kid. Did you know that you can make money with your brains? You could easily become a tutor or a paid teacher.

You can actually teach a variety of subjects. You probably don't realize that you can make great money teaching other kids musical instruments, coding, chess, art, sports, anything that you are really good and passionate about.

I'm not kidding either about sports. In the town I used to live in on Long Island, some teenagers got paid to give young boys 1-on-1 lacrosse lessons!

Another example, my sister is only 11 years old, but she's a piano teacher and has multiple students.

You may be shocked to discover that a parent would hire someone so young. But here's why a parent would pay you to teach their kids. They might think their child would respond better or be more inspired by an older child. Also, a kid is a lot cheaper than a professional.

Of course, there's also traditional school subjects that you can tutor in! Math presents the most opportunity. I know several math whiz teenagers who make up to $40 an hour teaching math to other kids!

Also, my cousin once told me that rich kids in her school paid her regularly to do their homework. Some people think this is unethical, but I'm not going to tell you where to draw your own moral boundaries. Just remember a couple things. President Obama didn't actually write any of his speeches. And your parents often exceed the legal speed limit on the highway. (LOL)

"When you teach, you learn twice." - Joseph Joubert

Tutoring is better than a lemonade stand because there is absolutely zero financial risk to yourself and because it's weather-proof.

Odd Jobs

"If opportunity doesn't knock, build a door." - Milton Berle

Desperate for some cash? Dust the neighbors china collection! Mow your Grandma's lawn! Rake leaves! Pick up sticks! Organize closets! (Yes, that is a thing.) Just make money! But seriously, you can make lots of money just by doing random jobs.

For example, dog walkers in NYC get paid $20-30 for a half hour, and some can do like 10 dogs at a time, so in other words, $400 an hour. Pretty sweet, huh? Of course there are other complications, but you can make a lot of money for taking Fido out for 20 minutes to poop.

Or you could hire yourself out as a housekeeper if you are really good at cleaning. I haven't personally tried this, as I am not good at cleaning, but if you can stomach it, cleaning out bathrooms is a great way to make money, because nobody else wants to do it.

If you're walking by your neighbor's house, and you see there are a ton of leaves in their front yard, offer to rake them. Instead of waiting for them to ask you, you have to bring their problems and your solutions to their attention.

If you get good at identifying problems and offering solutions, then you'll never be out of work - or money!

Sell Online

Why would you sell anything on the roadside....when you could sell online? I bet you can't find one thing in the economy that isn't sold online nowadays. There are snow plows, wedding rings, even a piece of cereal shaped like Abraham Lincoln's head all available!

The easiest thing to sell online is most undoubtedly your old toys and collectibles. Let's say you have a first edition Captain America figure. It's worthless to you, but it could actually be worth $50 to a collector. So what do you do? Put it up for sale on eBay or Craigslist. And don't stop there. Put everything you're not using up for sale! You'll be amazed at how much of your stuff gets sold.

You can also sell your old clothing on websites like Poshmark. Chances are, somebody's stupid enough to buy your out-of-vogue apparel. But really, people sell a lot of "NWT" clothing there - which means it's "new with tags" and has never even been worn. (The average person supposedly throws away 80 lbs of clothes each year!)

Also, you can liquidate other people's junk, too. Older people, like your grandparents, might not know that their old memorabilia has value, and some of them don't even know how to take and upload picture. You can sell it for them and earn a percentage of the sale!

You want to have as much up for sale as possible. Then you'll have more money flowing in.

Selling stuff online is better because people can order around the clock, which means you can make money while you eat, sleep, and poop!

Make Music

> *"Somebody said to me, 'But the Beatles were anti-materialistic.' That's a huge myth. John and I literally used to sit down and say, 'Now, let's write a swimming pool.'"* - *Paul McCartney*

Did you know that the music industry is worth $130 BILLION? Everybody likes some kind of music. There's constant demand for music all over the globe. Maybe you play a musical instrument or two. If so, then don't just sit on your talent. Use it to make money!

First of all, you can get paid to play at restaurants, retirement homes, and even churches. My 16 year old friend plays the organ at a church for $100 an hour! Pretty insane!

Second, if you can't get a scheduled gig, try "busking". This is where you go to a public place, put out a tip jar, and play music.

Finally, you could compose your own music with programs like MuseScore (free), GarageBand (also free), and Sibelius ($5 a year) and sell the rights to it.

So yes, you can use your musical skills to make money. And you can make lots of money doing something that you love! Making music is better than a lemonade stand because it can be a lot more fun!

Sell...Pumpkins?

This might sound crazy, but during the Halloween season... people actually want pumpkins! I mentioned how I sold pumpkins earlier, and people were snapping those things up like hot cakes!

And you don't have to just sell Halloween decorations. Is it Christmastime? Try to sell some wreaths, or even actual trees if you can pull that off. Easter? Sell some beautiful colored eggs door-to-door on the day before Easter! Parents who need eggs will be throwing money at your face.

These are called seasonal businesses, because they only operate during a certain time of year. They can be better than a lemonade stand, because some people get really fired up about the holidays and spend gobs of money!

I've given you a bunch of ways to make money that are way better than a lemonade stand. Now go try out as many as possible!

CHAPTER 9

YOUR FUTURE IS RIGHT NOW

In this chapter, I'm going to talk about some of the many money-making opportunities. After all, this is the Golden Age of entrepreneurship.

Robots

> *"I am fluent in over 6 million forms of communication."* - *C3PO*

Did you know that 38 percent of all jobs are at very high risk of being replaced by robots in the next 15 years? Crazy, huh?

At fast food places, employees are getting replaced by kiosks that take your order, not selfies. Janitors are being replaced by Roombas. Construction workers are being replaced by robotic cranes and wrecking balls. Even financial professionals are being replaced by software that will do your tax returns and make your investments cheaper and more effectively.

Why do you think all the tech leaders keep talking about drones and autonomous cars?

Because soon all the "driver" jobs will be gone too, maybe.

People have long thought that in the future, robots would do everything... and now finally they are being proven correct! So you better move your butt fast before Amazon robot drones start selling candy in your school! After all, it's only a matter of time before your parents get replaced by robots.

I'm just saying that maybe you should start tinkering with that LEGO Mindstorms or Arduino set you got, because after all, robots, VR, and all of these new technologies are where the big money is going to be made.

Globalization

"It's a small world (after all)..." - Disney ride/song

Back when your parents were kids, they couldn't easily call someone in India - Indians didn't have phones and it would have been too expensive. They definitely couldn't send them digital pictures, files, and messages. Basically, the people of the world were completely cut off from each other.

So what happened? Rapid technological progress happened. PCs crashed in price. The Internet was born. Bill Gates created Windows. Smartphones came to the masses. The whole world became able to communicate with each other and became totally connected.

For example, I just sent someone in Pakistan an image to edit/Photoshop! I could have done the job myself, but I was busy and it only cost me $6 to "outsource" this task and Pradeep did it perfectly in 20 minutes!

For the very first time in history, the whole world's resources are now available to you. Not only can you talk to somebody in India, you can hire them! I have a client who lives 2,500 miles away in Phoenix, Arizona!

Globalization isn't just about cheap labor and Skype-ing with your cousin in China. Globalization has given you access to a whole bunch of potential customers. Instead of selling your book and other products or services to just people in your own country or community, you can sell to 7 BILLION people all over the globe. Note that almost all businesses today have international footprints....it wasn't always like this.

Abundance

> *"We are racing toward a world of abundance, and we are going to be increasing the quality of life for everyone on this planet." - Peter Diamandis*

Do you know how much money there is in the world? There is $5 TRILLION traded in financial markets every single day! There is enough money for everyone to become wealthy.

Yet some people think getting rich is a zero-sum game, which means that if you win, everybody else loses. But they are wrong. There is a ridiculous amount of money out there. And guess what? It's all ripe for the picking! All you have to do is go get your share.

Educational resources are also unlimited. There are 2,000 episodes of just the EOFire podcast that can teach you all about entrepreneurship. And they're FREE!

Because of email and social media and all of these technological advances, you can now easily connect with anyone on Earth: authors, celebrities, CEOs, et al.

If you publish an article on LinkedIn and Tim Ferriss shares it, then 9 million people could see your post! This wasn't possible just a couple decades ago.

As you can see, the opportunities before you are infinite and abundant...

But do you know what isn't abundant? Time. Every second we have less time. Every second is gone forever. That means every second you waste is time you could be earning some of that money. Which is all the more reason you have to get rich right now!

The Tech Boom

"We're changing the world with technology." - Bill Gates

Humans have created absolutely amazing stuff straight out of a sci-fi movie. We can take a picture of a Frappuccino on a computer the size of a quarter and someone in Japan, 7,000 miles away, can see it! And every year business, inventors, and scientists create more and more futuristic technology!

Have you seen a 3D printer, or used one? Those things are mind blowing! You can literally make pretty much anything you want! Want to make a custom chess set? No problem! Just design it, and then print it!

And with each new revolutionary technology, there are new massive opportunities to make money. When the iPhone came out and millennials started dropping them in their toilets, somebody repaired waterlogged phones and made lots of money! Of course there was also millions to make in selling apps, phone cases (without Logan Paul on them), and headphones (think Beats).

So what's going to happen next? I don't know, but it will most definitely be a fantastic opportunity for you and me!

Tech is going to keep on booming....with or without you. That's why it's super-important that you try to stay on top of the latest gadgets, trends, and innovations in the tech world. Read the TechCrunch blog. Keep tabs on big events like CES (Consumer Electronics Show). Generally peel your ears and keep an open mind towards the new wacky stuff.

Industry Disruption

"Digital is the main reason just over half of the companies on the Fortune 500 have disappeared since the year 2000." - Pierre Nanterme

Do you know what an answering machine is?

You probably don't, because they've become obsolete, like horse buggy whips. But not long ago, answering machines were cutting edge technology. They were these devices that would record telephone messages left by people who would... well, I don't really know what they are either. But in 1990, half of all American households used one! What happened to them?

iPhones happened. All of a sudden, nobody needed an answering machine because the phones would do the mysterious, forgotten task of the answering machine, and they would do it even better.

This is a classic example of industry disruption. A classic example of a new innovation rendering another one totally obsolete.

Do you know what a Polaroid camera is? It's another casualty of the iPhone. Now, nobody uses an instant camera because they have one built-in on their phone.

Because technological breakthroughs are constantly disrupting every single industry on Earth, there are tons of new money-making opportunities for kids around the globe. It wasn't always like this. Ask your parents and grandparents! They used to fight with other kids over the lone paper route in the neighborhood.

When the iPhone was invented, there was money to be made coding iPhone apps. I've mentioned Thomas Suarez, Robert Nay, and Palmer Luckey before. They took advantage of this brand new industry.

Netflix disrupted the film industry.

Blogs, websites, and social media disrupted the traditional media industry - newspapers, magazines, television, etc.

Google, YouTube, Udemy, Khan Academy, Wikipedia, and a million others have disrupted education. (Video games have too, but not in the same positive way. LOL.)

Basically every single industry had been upended by changes in tech.

So get ready, because the next great industry disruption is about to happen. In fact, it may be…

Voice Technology

> *"Our 2017 projections for Alexa were very optimistic, and we far exceeded them.... We don't see positive surprises of this magnitude very often - expect us to double down." - Jeff Bezos*

Do you know what the Amazon Echo is? Probably. You might even have one! In case you don't know, it's a voice-activated "smart speaker" that plays music, sets alarms, tells you the weather, and a whole bunch of other things. You can also download "Skills" on it that are like "apps" for your Alexa. For example, one skill lets you play Jeopardy!, and another plays soothing sounds as you go to bed.

So what does this have to do with making money? Remember how much money the kids I just mentioned made fixing iPhones and creating apps? Well, Alexa Skills could be the new App Store.

There's also the Google Home, which was Google's attempt to make their own smart speaker. Personally, I think it will be even more successful than the Alexa. Of course, there's Apple's Siri, Samsung's Bixby, and a host of other intelligent assistants. I know a lot about this because I have a client who works in this space. If you are looking for a fantastic resource when it comes to voice technology, then check out the podcasts on VoiceFirst.FM!

Soon, people will be able to do anything just by saying it. Heck, soon we won't even have to leave our seats to do anything. You'll just say, "Alexa, order Burger King." and then a drone will deliver the food to you through a window in your house that you command to open.

So what can you do? Well, you can learn how to make Alexa Skills so you won't be left behind in voice technology in case it really takes off. There are tons of free courses on it, like at Codecademy.com. It's actually pretty easy, and it's easier if you already know how to code.

Consider All Opportunities

> *"I could either watch it happen or be a part of it." - Elon Musk*

The next big thing might not be voice technology.

It might be artificial intelligence - "AI" - but they've been hyping that for decades actually. My Dad said he wrote a paper on how AI was the next BIG thing way back in 1987! (LOL)

It might be drone technology. Have you seen those selfie drones that follow you around and can snap pics of you? Have you seen those way cool Drone Racing League videos?

It might be "blockchain", which I don't know a ton about, but it's a very hyped-up new technology related to Bitcoin and all of these other cryptocurrencies. You and I would be stupid not to take a closer look.

It might be the "Internet of Things", which refers to all your appliances connecting to the internet and talking to each other. Supposedly your alarm clock will go off and by the time you get to the shower, the hot water will already be turned on.

My Dad came across Netscape early on in the mid 90s but said he totally dismissed it. If he hadn't, maybe he'd have seen that it was the future (internet browsing), invested in the stock, made millions, and I wouldn't have to work so hard for him now!

My Dad also said he underestimated Facebook. He could have used it to grow his business. He also could have bought the stock for a lot cheaper, before it exploded. He dismissed it because he thought it was a stupid waste of time. He didn't look it with an open mind and from a business standpoint.

But my Dad wanted me to say that he did buy Google early on (at around a hundred dollars a share). Because he was using it a lot, he sensed the potential of its business model and growth. (We sold our shares just now at over $2,000 each!)

If you want to get super-rich, you have to be aware of all the new technologies cropping up. Don't do what my father did! All you have to do is spot the next big thing early on and you can be set for life!

The Golden Age of Entrepreneurship

> *"The golden age is before us, not behind us." - William Shakespeare*

As you now know, today is the best time in history, EVER, for aspiring *Kid Trillionaires.*

I hope this chapter, and the whole book, is getting you excited about the bazillion ways you can start making money today. I'm getting more excited myself just by writing this book! Millionaires are being minted in an instant because of these technological breakthroughs. I hope you're next.

CHAPTER 10

THE SECRET WEAPONS

Getting rich is definitely not a video game, but there are indeed "powerups" that can accelerate your *Kid Trillionaire* journey. Here they are:

Magical Books

I've mentioned them already, but books can be some of the most powerful tools for building your fortune. When you find the right business or motivational book, it's like your elf druid finds a spellbook and learns a new spell that makes him do double damage or something.

Many people have said that Tim Ferriss' book, *The Four-Hour Workweek*, has changed their lives and made them a fortune. Others credit authors Tony Robbins, Dan Kennedy (my Dad's favorite), and Napoleon Hill with their success.

You might not like to read, but have you ever been in a summer reading program where you get prizes for reading books? Well, imagine making $2,000 just by implementing something you read in a book. That's a prize even the most book-hating kid would swallow their hatred for. A single book can make you rich! Actually, a single idea from a book can make you rich! That's why it's extra important to read as much as you can.

There will be a list of my favorite, most helpful books at the end of this one.

Profitable Connections

Another secret that can throw rocket fuel on your *Trillionaire* bonfire is other people. I'm talking about creating personal relationships with other human beings who can give you jobs, opportunities, and encouragement.

It's pretty obvious. Who can open more doors for you? Smelly Stevie NoName from your 6th grade class, or the mayor of the town?

For example, in the Long Island town my mother grew up in, everyone worked on Wall Street. Many of my Mom's classmates landed lucrative jobs when they got older, but not through the regular application process. Their aunt, uncle, parents, friends, or neighbors made a phone call and hooked them up!

In fact, my Mom just got my cousin a summer job on Wall Street with her connections!

Many people think this is unfair, and they whine about this injustice called "nepotism", but it doesn't matter. The reality is that personal connections in this world have and always will matter.

If you want to get rich, you need to start strategically growing your own social network.

Most kids do not think about this one bit. They only hang out with other boys and girls their own age in their own town. And this is definitely a skill that no school anywhere is teaching in its Common Core.

So how can you connect with people? Well, LinkedIn is a great place to start. It's technically a social media site for grown-ups, but you can sign up anyway. Nobody really cares. You just have to make your profile sound professional. If you have a business, write that you are "Founder and CEO of (your business here)". Check out my profile to see what I'm talking about.

Come to think of it….all of my current clients found me through personal connections!

Young Legs

Because we're kids, we have massive advantages over ~~fossils~~ older people who try to make money. For starters, we're cute. Grown-ups love to buy lemonade and raffle tickets from kids just because they're young! So we should milk that advantage before we hit puberty and start to smell.

Second, we can afford to mess up. We don't have as many responsibilities as older people do. We don't have any taxes to pay or mouths to feed. If your fidget spinner business fails, it won't be the end of the world.

Finally, we aren't afraid of anything. We are actually only born with two fears: the fear of falling, and the fear of loud sounds. As we get older, we acquire more fears, like that of being rejected, public speaking, and great white sharks at the beach. If we're not careful, we'll grow up and be too afraid to knock on someone's door and sell things. But now, we're practically invincible. So take full advantage of your youth!

More Time

Right now, you have way more free time than you ever will. It might be less than you had a couple years ago, but it's definitely going to continue to shrink as you get older and get more homework.

You see, when billionaires were kids, they used their "free time" to make mountains of money. They didn't waste any of it. You have to do the same.

There's a saying in the entrepreneurial world, "Everyone's got the same 24 hours in a day....We make time for what we truly want."

So if you really want to become a *Kid Trillionaire*, invest your free time in money-making activities.

The WWW

The birth of the internet was like a nuclear explosion. It blew everything up, but in a good way. It connected people all across the globe. It gave everybody instant access to the world's entire treasure of information. It's also armed the entire world with powerful tools of creation, like Blogger and Canva. And it's basically free.

The amount of things you can to do to make money on the internet is nearly unlimited. You can sell things, create websites, turn yourself into a celebrity, connect with powerful people, research and write books (like *Kid Trillionaire*)...anything!

You can use the internet to learn a new skill. With Google, Udemy, YouTube, and all of these fantastic resources, you can discover anything.

You can get your business idea or invention funded by Kickstarter or GoFundMe...

You can also do work on the internet. All of my client work is done via the WWW. I transcribe podcasts, use Adobe cloud-based software, run marketing campaigns, share files on Dropbox, send emails, and manage social media accounts. None of this would be possible for me, a kid, without the internet! I'm vertically challenged so I'd have to be a chimney sweep or something…

You must make full use of the bounty of the web….because your strongest competitors definitely will be.

Self-Motivation

We've covered motivation in a few earlier chapters. Here I just wanted to stress again how all-important it is. Without motivation, you simply will not make money. Period. Forget *Trillionaire*, you'll remain a *Kid Nillionaire*.

But if you can become fanatically self-driven, you can achieve almost

ANYTHING you aim for - and probably a whole lot more!

Remember, use visual aids. My Dad's dream is to open his school on the top of the World Trade Center in New York City. So he changed the wallpaper on all of his devices to a beautiful picture of the skyscraper!

When you need help with your motivation, and everyone does at times…

Go to YouTube and watch "motivational videos", like from Caleb Maddix, Grant Cardone, Tony Robbins, and Earl Nightingale! Create a playlist of your favorites. After one (or ten!) of those, you will be beating your chest and feeling like you can do anything.

You could also blast your favorite music to get your mojo flowing! Many famous speakers do this before they have to make a big speech. I learned about this from Steve Chandler, a coach and motivation guru.

Motivation is like having an angry bull chasing you while you run a marathon. You will run like you've never before and get to the finish line before anyone else.

Increasing Scale

According to Investopedia, scale is "a company's capability to grow without being hampered by its structure or available resources." In other words, it's referring to your business' or businesses' ability to grow.

When you have a normal, run-of-the-mill lemonade stand, there's a hard limit to the amount of money you can make. You might be set up in the sunniest, most popular spot of the park, but you still can't sell lemonade every day of the year, to the entire town - never mind the next town over!

It's like when you are playing a shooting game and you only have a slow-loading, single-shot pistol. There's no way you can take down the entire massive horde of zombies before they get to you.

But let's say you made a whole bunch of lemonade stands and hired cute kids to man them. All of a sudden, you have a gatling gun and can massacre the entire undead mob in an instant.

This is an example of increasing the scale of your business.

Right now, I'm super busy with client work. I'm trading a lot of my time for dollars. The only way I can add scale is to charge more or to work more hours. So I'm trying to figure out how I can increase the scale of my business and free up more time for myself.

No matter what business you go into, you should constantly be thinking about how you can increase its scale. That's how you're going to get filthy rich.

Overdelivery

Kid Trillionaire emphasizes money and aggression. BUT you still always have to provide a great product or amazing service to your customers and clients. Here's why:

When you deliver a fantastic product, the customer will be more likely to buy from you again, and again and again and again. This might seem obvious, but you'd be surprised at how much goodwill is generated by going the extra mile. You can do this by giving them unexpected bonuses, being polite, handwritten thank-you notes, etc.

Secondly, when you give them a great service, they'll tell their friends about you. And their friends will tell their friends and on and on and on. You'll automatically gain new customers!

Unfortunately, this is not true if you are a babysitter. If Sally babysits for Mr. and Mrs. Smith and overdelivers…

If she does the dishes, reads to the kids, and is really cheap, then there is no way Mr. and Mrs. Smith are going to tell their best friends about Sally. There's no way they are going to refer her to anyone else because they don't want to try to go out one Friday night only to discover that Sally has been "poached" by their best friends, who pay her more!

> *"Overdeliver in all you do and soon you will be rewarded for the extra effort." - Zig Ziglar*

Multiple Money Streams

Your road to becoming a *Kid Trillionaire* is a lot faster when you have a bunch of different businesses making money for you all at once.

Like maybe you have set up a pinball machine in a barber shop à la Warren Buffett, you sell candy in school, you teach guitar, you babysit, you mow your grandmother's lawn, and it's that time of year so you're selling Christmas decorations too.

Having your own mini-conglomerate guarantees you will always have work because it's unlikely that you lose all of those customers at the same time. It protects you against bad luck, competition, people moving, etc.

The other great thing about having multiple money streams is that you'll clearly see which businesses you enjoy and which ones have the most upside - so you'll know where it's best to focus your attention.

> *"The worst number in business is 1." - Dan Kennedy*

What Dan is saying is that you never want to be dependent on 1 of anything: one business, one customer, one product or service, one method of advertising, or even one supplier. Because it's 100% certain that things won't always stay the same - no matter how good things are going for you right now.

Master Marketing

It doesn't matter how good your stuff is if nobody knows about it. You could even have the very best product at the very best price in the whole entire world, but you'll still fail if you don't advertise and market effectively.

A common complaint among non-rich people is that "I'm a better ______ than her! Why does she make more money than me?" What they don't understand is the supremacy of marketing.

"Obscurity is your biggest problem." - Grant Cardone

Have you seen the Squatty Potty YouTube video? The one with unicorns pooping out rainbow soft-serve ice cream? It went viral and has been viewed 33 MILLION times! That is a real triumph of marketing. Just think how many more Squatty Potties have been sold because of that hilarious video - which was FREE to post on YouTube.

Future *Kid Trillionaires* understand that 80% of any business success is pure marketing. Therefore they will devote 80% of their time to passing out flyers, publishing articles online, handing out business cards, writing a book like this(!), improving their image, and making offers.

The art and science of mastering marketing has so many components, I couldn't possibly cover them all in this book. There's lead generation advertising, postal mail, email marketing, referral marketing, newsletters, internet marketing, anti-social media, television, radio ads, lions and tigers and bears oh my! If you want to become a *Kid Trillionaire*, it's imperative that you become a serious student of marketing. My Dad and I study anything and everything on this subject by Dan Kennedy. You should too!

Goals

Among the super-successful, there's a skill above all other skills. It's the ability to set and accomplish personal goals.

This isn't about "dreaming". Even the laziest people on Earth dream about owning fancy jewelry, big homes, fast cars, and hundred dollar bills, y'all.

It takes no effort to just imagine. But if you don't take any action towards your dreams, then they stay just that - dreams. When you have a clear goal and a plan to achieve it, your whole body and mind will work around-the-clock and very hard towards this goal.

Choose your goals wisely. I don't want to discourage you from your ambitious goals, but you can't be crazy. If you aim too high, your lack of progress will discourage you and you'll quit. Don't say you want to become a pro basketball player if you are short, slow, and always the last kid picked in gym class. Don't set out to be the next American Idol if you objectively sing like a bullfrog.

If you pick goals that you really, really want to attain, they will automatically motivate you to not only do the hard work that is necessary... But also to bulldoze through any and all obstacles.

Once you've figured out what you really want, you've got to come up with a comprehensive plan to put that Lamborghini in your driveway. So how do you do it? You actually start backwards.

Say you want to write a book and have it in stores by the Christmas season. Obviously, you have to send it to the printer by Halloween. That means it must be completely written and edited by then. And if you want it to be 10 chapters long, and it's January, that means you must write a chapter a month. So now you have a clear idea on how much work it's going to take and whether you're on track to achieve your goal or not at all times.

A big goal will always have these micro-targets beneath it. After all, if you want to lose 20 pounds in two months, you can't lose 19 pounds on the last day!

Once you set a goal, no matter how high, you'll be amazed at how ideas, money, resources, and people materialize out of nowhere to aid you.

> *"When you want something, all the universe conspires in helping you achieve it." - Paulo Coelho*

CHAPTER 11

IF YOU SIT ON YOUR BUTT...

What happens if you don't make money as a kid? What happens if you coast through life, just playing sports, watching TV, and studying hard at school?

You might think that because your parents pay for all your clothes, your movie tickets, your new iPhone X, your theme park visits, and your everything....that you don't need to make money now. But if you don't start learning how to get rich, you'll miss out on how much more amazing your life can be today. You'll also put your entire future seriously at risk.

This wasn't the most fun part of the book to write, and I don't think it will be the most fun part for you to read. But I have to include this section to be brutally honest with you about what's at stake. Because after all, your teachers and your friends are not going to warn you.

Meet Penniless Peter. He didn't do a single thing to make money his whole life. Now he's 24. He's...

Dirt Poor

Peter is broke. He can't go out to dinner. He can barely pay his rent. He can't buy presents for his family at Christmas. He has a flip phone. He couldn't go see the new Star Wars movie, even though he was looking forward to it all year.

Obviously, nobody really wants to be poor. Nobody likes having to use a flip phone – except for Grandma. Nobody likes not being to afford the newest Xbox. Whenever Peter sees an advertisement for a game, phone, restaurant, or car, it's saying to him, "No, not for you. You're poor!" Peter is also a...

Perma-Moocher

> *"I don't want no scrub....Hangin' out the passenger side....Of his best friend's ride." - TLC*

Peter would starve to death if it wasn't for two things: the government, and his parents. Embarrassingly, Peter pays for food with the handouts he gets from the government and his parents. And he's lucky to have a part-time job at a fast food restaurant, as boring and demeaning as it is. Otherwise, he wouldn't be able to pay his rent or bring french fries home for dinner. If he got fired or laid off, he would have to move back into his parents' basement yet again.

Who would want to always depend on their parents for money? How embarrassing is that? And what happens if the government stops giving Peter money? What would he do? What if his parents stopped giving him money? Or he got replaced by an automatic kiosk at his job? He would starve! And Peter has to suffer the shame of being...

De-Friended

Peter has zero friends, unless you count his coworker Steve, who always smells like moldy cheese and sounds like an angry gerbil whenever he talks. Peter's probably Steve's only friend, as well.

Why does Peter have no friends? Because Peter can't go out to dinner with potential friends, and he doesn't have a big screen TV that his possible friends could watch on Super Bowl night. Peter is as fun as a brick trampoline, because he's broke.

Who wants to be friends with a penniless loser? Nobody except other penniless losers. And that's a fantastic crowd to hang out with. (NOT.)

Fall Behind

"And those who fall behind get beaten…" - Joseph Stalin

Peter's old college friends have leapt far ahead of him. They all have fantastic desk jobs at Google, or they work for themselves. They all have nicer cars and big apartments in the hippest neighborhoods. They are living the life, eating filet mignon at Le Fancy Steakhouse whenever they want. Meanwhile Peter subsists on 19¢ ramen noodle packets. The chicken flavor, to be precise.

And even though Peter has been working hard for 2 years, he can't even get a promotion to chief burger flipper. He probably needs to go back to Chapter 3 and read about dead end jobs. It's utterly painful to watch his "old" friends get so far ahead of him. He feels like he can never catch up - and so he's stopped trying.

Deflated by Inflation

You may have noticed that the prices of everything go up every single year. Or you might not have noticed, because you are young. But go ask your parents how much it cost for them to buy a candy bar or go to the movies when they were kids.

When my Dad was a child, he remembers paying as low as 25¢ for a candy bar and even as low as $2.25 for the movies (E.T. in 1982). But today, a candy bar costs nearly 5 times as much, and movie tickets cost $9 - and that doesn't include the rip-off popcorn! In NYC where I live, a movie ticket costs $14!

This is called inflation, and it happens because the government prints more money every day and therefore all existing money becomes worth less. So if you sit on your butt, making little-to-no coin each year, everything you dream of buying....gets more and more expensive and further and further out of reach. Remember, whether you're working or not, inflation is working hard against you.

Can't Help Anyone

Peter's parents have taken care of him his whole life. They spent tens of thousands of dollars of their hard-earned money for him to go to theme parks, go on vacations, and for his braces. They even used their own retirement funds to pay for his college degree in Advanced Millennial Gaming Technology.

Now they're way past their peak earning years. They're old and on a fixed income. They don't have any money saved up, because, again, they spent it all on Peter.

He's really grateful for everything they've done, and that's why he feels terrible that not only he can't help them now, but that he's still a parasite.

Unhealthy

Peter can't really afford organic green smoothies for lunch, unlike all of his healthy peers. He's been reduced to eating off of the dollar menu at McDonalds every single day. He pays with loose change, too.

Peter also has no time to exercise, because he's working 80 hours a week at that dead end job. He's always exhausted when his shift is over, and doesn't feel like doing burpees and hitting the Stairmaster at the YMCA. Instead...

He self-medicates his sadness with donuts and Coca-Cola. After all, who's going to drown their sorrows with a bowl of kale?

He's an Embarrassment

Peter's parents like to forget about him. They're always inviting his brother,

Rich Roger to family events, but Peter always gets "accidentally" left out. It's pretty sad. His relatives don't like to admit it, but Peter is the shame of the family. They even paid someone to photoshop Peter out of the family picture. They do theoretically love him, but he's just so embarrassing!

When you are poor, you might become the black sheep of the family. Your more successful siblings will be the pride and joy, but you will just be the "forgotten one". But when you are rich, you'll be the one in the limelight!

Depressed

Peter feels down all the time about everything. He skipped his high school's 5-year reunion because he didn't want to see all of his old classmates. He didn't want to have to answer questions about what he's been doing.

He doesn't like to log on to Facebook or Instagram either, because all he sees is his peers with their smiling faces, fabulous vacations, and perfect lives. No matter where he looks and where he goes, he's reminded of his failures.

Apparently, someone making less than $24,000 a year is twice as likely to be depressed as someone making over $60,000 a year. Pretty scary, right? Everyone knows that money doesn't guarantee happiness, but that doesn't mean that being broke will make you happy. If that was true, about 40% of America would be singing for joy.

When Peter actually does think a little....he thinks that his life would be so much happier if he could just figure out how to make some more coin!

Stressed Out

Peter is constantly worried about the future.

He doesn't know how he's going to pay the next bill. He's worried that one of his college buddies will see him flipping burgers. He's worried about making his next minimum credit card payment. He's worried his landlord is going to raise his rent. He's worried that McDonald's will remove the Dollar

Menu. He's worried the price of gas is going to keep going up. He's worried he's going to get hurt, because he can't afford health insurance.

He's worried he might get replaced by a burger flipping robot, just like his coworker Steve. He's worried he's going to lose all of the money he ~~invested~~ gambled in that shady cryptocurrency. He's worried that he'll never have a girlfriend, never mind get married and have a family. But other than all of these trivial concerns and a dozen more, he's perfectly fine!

Stuck

Peter would like to travel to a bunch of places. He'd love to go skiing in Colorado. He wants to hit the sunny beaches of Florida. He'd like to go to those head-banging concerts like his former college buddies do. But these are just the pipe dreams of a wage slave.

He doesn't have the time to even take a couple days off, he doesn't have any friends to go with, and he can't even afford a one-way ticket to any of these places.

Peter is flat-out stuck where he is. They say money can't solve every problem, but it would definitely help solve this one!

Time's a Ticking

Peter was a happy kid with a bright future just a short time ago. He blinked his eyes, he woke up, and is already 24. Now he's broke, dependent on others, lonely, and at the rear of the pack. He feels miserable about his family and his future. If he doesn't do something drastic now, he'll be forever broke. Don't be like Peter.

CHAPTER 12

TRILLIONAIRE NINJA TACTICS

We've covered the basics. I've certainly given you a lot to chew on. Now it's time for me to reveal the most potent, advanced level tools and tactics.

Hoard Dollars

> *"Greed, for lack of a better word, is good." - Gordon Gekko*

You already know you need to make and accumulate a little money. But the thing is, *Kid Trillionaires* will save nearly every single penny that touches their hands!

If you spend money the second you earn it (or even before you get it), then it doesn't matter how much you bring in. You may as well have not worked at all - at least then you would still have had your time!

Everyone has things that they have always wanted to buy. And when they finally can afford them, it's really hard to resist. When I first started earning some decent money, I would spend it on books, and more lately, Yu-Gi-Oh! cards. I'm not saying those things are a total waste of money. But you could instantly blow all of your cash on impulse buys unless you create a habit of saving first, like Warren Buffett, one of the richest men in the world.

> *"Do not save what is left after spending, but spend what is left after saving." - Warren Buffett*

I opened a PayPal account, and asked my clients to pay me on PayPal instead. I'm able to receive money, but I can't spend it - my Dad says he'll "murderize" me. So my account only grows. I have nearly $2,000 as of this moment and I only started doing this about 5 months ago. (By the time you are reading this book….I'll have a whole lot more, bank on that!).

So when you make money, get it out of your wallet and into a piggy bank, or even better, a real bank, real fast. This way it's a lot harder for you to spend it. You might even forget about it, and one day you'll look at it and see a massive, beautiful number that needs commas.

Put Your Money To Work

> *"Schools teach you how to work for money, but don't teach how to make money work for you." - Robert Kiyosaki*

First of all, once you start hoarding money, put it in a bank. Why? It's safer, from yourself, your thievin' siblings, anyone who might be rooting around in your house (like the maid), and also because you can earn interest on it.

In a bank account, your money increases each year by a percentage (right now, as high as 1.75%). The interest rates are pretty low right now, but history tells us that they will go back up soon. When my Dad started saving, you could earn 5% a year without doing anything!

While interest might seem insignificant, it's better than nothing, and as you sock away more money....you'll be amazed at how earning interest accelerates your wealth.

> *"Compound interest is the eighth wonder of the world. He who understands it, earns it ... he who doesn't ... pays it." - Albert Einstein*

Another way you can put money to work is to reinvest your profits back into in your business. For example, McDonald's founder Ray Kroc invested every single penny he earned into expanding his business all across America. Phil Knight did the same with Nike. For years, they didn't make any money at all. Recently, Jeff Bezos' Amazon is the best example of a company reinvesting in itself to the maximum. And obviously, that has paid off big-time!

Say you have an upstart little lawn mowing business, and you make a few hundred bucks. You could put that money under your mattress, in a bank, or you could use it to get a bigger and faster lawnmower that helps you make even more money!

Obviously, there are many other "investments" you could make to turn your little pile of cash into a big pile of cash, such as the stock market, commodities, bonds, even cryptocurrencies. The problem is, it's hard for kids and adults to tell whether or not those investments are actually risky gambles. That's why in this book, I'm only going to recommend the safest investments - that would be in the bank, in your own business, and in yourself (to be elaborated upon in a bit).

Increase Leverage

> *"Financial leverage is the advantage the rich have over the poor and middle class." - Robert Kiyosaki*

Do you know what the concept of leverage is? It's exerting only a little effort... but making a HUGE impact. It's like moving the Earth with Archimedes' lever.

So what exactly is a company with financial leverage? Well, it could be having a monopoly, a business with no competition. For example, go to Disney, order lunch, and your eyes will pop out at $11 for a small, cheeseless burger!

Disney can charge you whatever it wants, because you're trapped in their park!

It could also be having a truly unique product. There's only one Super Bowl that the whole world watches, right? That's why they can charge 5 million dollars for a 30-second TV commercial.

Obviously you can't build a theme park or compete with the NFL championship, but there's still many tiny but powerful things you can do to insulate yourself from competition and charge a pretty penny for your products.

You could become famous with a celebrity endorsement or even a popular video. For example, I was in a video that went viral on YouTube and has 1.2 million views. Now, random people come up to me at chess tournaments in New York, New Jersey, Connecticut, and even Tennessee(!) and say, "Hey, you were the kid in that Cornbread video!" It also helped me gain many, many subscribers for my website, KidsGetRich.com.

So let's say that I spoke at some big event for an hour and made $20,000! That's about what most people make in a whole year! And I only worked for an hour! Now, who's to say that you couldn't do that? Remember, Caleb Maddix is doing that right now! (BTW, I'm going to do a speaking tour with this book.)

Leverage is awesome. Figure out how to use it for your business, and you'll be richer than you can imagine.

Hire Helpers

> *"Do what you do best, and outsource the rest." - Peter Drucker*

There are almost zero ultra-successful people and businesses that don't have any employees. It's hard to grow anything real big as a "solopreneur" or all on your own.

We've already talked about adding scale and leverage to your business, and that's exactly what the right other people can do for you.

Here are some of the good things that will happen if and when you start hiring helpers.

They can free you up from doing stuff that you don't really want to do. For example, you don't see restaurant owners cleaning the toilets in the bathrooms. They're doing other more important things!

Hiring workers fills holes in your business. For example, you could hire a terrific graphic designer, who'll make better images than you will. You could hire a 13-year-old kid to do all your websites, funnels, payment integrations, audio editing, graphic design, video FX and pay him practically nothing, like my Dad does. Man, I need to get a raise!

Helpers can also dramatically improve the profitability of your business. If you hire a salesperson who is as good as you, you'll double your sales! Imagine what hiring 10 salespeople could do for your business.

Finally, making money is more fun when you do it with your own team. Warren Buffett worked with Charlie Munger for practically his whole life. Bill Gates founded Microsoft with Paul Allen. Mark Zuckerberg founded it with his classmates and Sean Parker.

> *"The reality is you cannot have a great business if it's just you. You need to add other people. If you don't believe me, try to name one truly great business that is successful, ongoing, viable, and growing that doesn't have many people making it happen." - Grant Cardone*

Anticipate Gold Rushes

> *"...get busy on the next great thing." - Steve Jobs*

When it comes down to it, there are a couple big categories of ways to make money. One, make something new that people want. Two, take something old that people wanted....and make it better. Three, spot the next new big thing early on and ride the wave. The big money is in number three.

Do you know why Michael Dell is worth $23.6 BILLION? Because he had the ability to see the future. He predicted that the prices of personal computers (PCs) would keep falling and he built that into his business model - unlike his competitors.

Erik Finman is 19 years old, and he's a millionaire. How? When he was younger, his grandmother gave him $1,000. Instead of blowing it on random junk like most teenagers would, he invested it in this new thing called Bitcoin. Bitcoin was worth around $12 when he bought them. Guess how much a single Bitcoin is worth now? $9,400!

Remember Andrew Carnegie's story? He saw that steel was going to be the next big thing, and he took advantage of that foresight to become one of the world's richest men.

When you can accurately anticipate gold rushes, you can make gobs of money really fast, really easily. And remember, one of the best ways to do that is, instead of digging for gold, to "sell picks and shovels" to other prospectors.

Notice that almost all of the success stories in this book are about people who somehow capitalized on big shifts in the economy - even if accidentally.

Heed Economic History

> *"You've got to find out the history of people who've tried your idea....because there's a 99.9999% chance your idea has been tried before." - Mark Cuban*

Have you ever come up with a really stupid business idea - like selling ice to Eskimos? Did your parents calmly try to explain to you why it wouldn't work, or did they just shake their heads and call you an idiot? Take a wild guess what my Dad does...

It's definitely important to have crazy, visionary ideas like what Elon Musk is famous for...

But you'd be foolish to look towards the future without studying the past. After all, nothing exists in a vacuum. If you learn the history of industries, "bubbles", market crashes, currencies, and technology, you'll be better able to anticipate those gold rushes of easy money.

On the other hand, learning a little economic history can prevent you from making mistakes and getting sucked into potential disasters. My Dad was at a chess tournament in Brooklyn, and there was this loud guy there bragging about how investing in Bitcoin and cryptocurrencies was "free money". He even said he was making more money than his Wall Street friends. This was right before it dropped like a stone from its high (-75% in February 2017).

Don't just watch YouTube and read current business blogs. Read the classics, like *The Richest Man in Babylon* and *Reminiscences of a Stock Broker*, and you'll discover that the principles in them hold true even today! That's because the fundamental laws of business never change. I'm sure you've heard your social studies teacher say "history repeats itself" or something along those lines. It's true!

Without a doubt, future *Kid Trillionaires* will follow the golden paths already laid down by the most successful and richest people in history.

Earn Passive Income

> *"If you don't find a way to make money while you sleep, you work until you die." - Warren Buffett*

There are two ways to make money. There's active income, which requires you to show up at a job, sell something, or generally trade your time for dollars. This is the way 99% of people earn money.

And then there's the vastly superior - passive income which only a tiny micro-fraction of people get to enjoy. That's when you make money without giving up your time. You wake up each day and your bank account just magically keeps growing. Examples of passive income would be earning interest from the bank, dividends from investments, rent from property you own, royalties from books you sell, or patents from your inventions.

Why is passive income better than active income? Well, imagine you're an investment banker on Wall Street. You're making $2 million a year. Pretty nice, right? But you have to work until 9pm every week, and all through the weekends. You don't get to see your family, and you can't ever go out on the fancy yacht you bought. That's why active income stinks. If you work too much, you won't even get to enjoy the rewards of it.

Some people say that $1 of passive income is equivalent to $3 in active income! How, you ask? Because passive income doesn't just let you sit at the beach and veg out. It also frees you up to grow your business and even start totally new ventures!

One of the main reasons I wrote this book was to create a passive income stream for myself. It was tiring doing hourly work for my clients.

Lucky for you, there's a great website called SmartPassiveIncome that can teach you all about how to make money while you eat, sleep, and poop.

Write A Book!

> *"The book that will most change your life is the book you write." - Seth Godin*

Writing a book is a great way to make money. I've already mentioned how Caleb Maddix and Emily Shai have earned gobs of money with their books. They are hardly alone. Tim Ferriss built his whole empire and personal brand on the success of one book - *The Four-Hour Workweek*. And of course JK Rowling made hundreds of millions writing the *Harry Potter* series.

Obviously I've made money writing a book too, if you or your parents bought this masterpiece. If you stole it....I'm coming to get you!

Writing a whole book may seem daunting but it isn't that hard, contrary to popular belief. Have you seen the *Diary of a Wimpy Kid* books? They're awesome - and I've actually met Jeff Kinney - but there ain't much there!

Write about something you know a lot about to start. Emily wrote her book on how to have a good sleepover! That's something anyone can just look up, but she still made $20,000 with it.

Or write a book on a topic that you know will sell. I chose to write *Kid Trillionaire* because I KNEW that the cover, the title, and the fact that I'm 13 alone would produce sales.

Don't write a book for kids titled *School and Vegetables Rule!*, because no one will buy that.

Write books about farts, pranks, zombie apocalypses, and teenage vampire love triangles, because there seems to be a huge appetite for those genres. What can I say but "LCD"! (Revisit your math textbook for that reference.)

There are many formulas and best practices on how to write a book. The outline is very important. Make sure you get very clear about that BEFORE you even begin writing. You can "speak" your book out and record it, and someone in Asia who doesn't speak English will transcribe it for one dollar, or a little more.

Dude/dudette, just write a book. It's going to do so much for you and your *Kid Trillionaire* journey.

Grab Land

> *"Well, real estate is always good, as far as I'm concerned."* - *Donald Trump*

You may have heard the term "real estate" thrown about. Maybe your parents work in real estate. But I'm going to tell you what it is in words that you will understand.

Real estate is land. People who buy and sell real estate just basically buy and sell land. Sometimes the land has a house or building on it, sometimes it doesn't. So what does real estate have to do with making money?

Somebody told my Dad years ago that real estate is the ultimate investment. They said because it has a "yield" and because it's protected against "inflation". We already talked about what inflation is. It's the tendency of prices to slowly and constantly rise. Yield means that you can rent your real estate out and earn money each month. For example if you buy a house, you can live in it, or you can rent it to another family for thousands of dollars a month.

My grandpa used to do this. He bought apartment buildings in Brooklyn way back in the 1970s when the rents were only about $300 a month. Over many years, the rents rose to almost $2,000 per month! In other words, his yield just went up over 6 times.

Here's another example. About twenty years ago, cell phones started to become popular for the first time. All of these companies needed to add cell towers on the tops of tall buildings to improve reception. My Dad knows a guy who jumped on this new development and brokered deals between tall building owners and companies like Verizon and Sprint. This guy was rewarded with millions of dollars for spotting this emerging trend.

That example might have been tough for a kid to pull off, but here's one that wasn't and might even have been way, way, way more profitable! Did you know that back in the early 90s, when the WWW was in its infancy, you could buy any ".com" domain name for like $10? If you had been alive back then, you could have bought cars.com or cellphones.com or videogames.com for practically nothing....and sold them for tens of millions of dollars today!

Here's a tip. If you see a kid in your class who's really good at sports or singing and is bound to be a star, ask them their name. Say her name is Emily Pimplefrump or something.

You should go online and try to snag EmilyPimplefrump.com now for $10-$12. Then when she's famous and really rich, she'll buy it back from you for thousands of dollars! People who buy and sell website addresses like this are called "domainers", and the earliest ones are incredibly rich and never have to work another day in their life.

Obviously, you probably can't buy a building, a farm, or a house to rent out. I wouldn't even recommend it if you could. But it's important to understand the power of real estate in wealth and business building. No matter what you do, whether it's a lemonade stand, or naming your website, you have to think about carving out a cornerstone property that has a lot of value based on its location.

Survey All Industries

> *"Realize that everything connects to everything else." - Leonardo da Vinci*

The global economy is truly massive.

You may have heard the word "industry" before, but what does it really mean? Quite simply, an industry is a slice or section of the larger economy.

Medicine is an industry. There are all sorts of pharmaceutical companies out there, making billions. Entertainment is an industry. Actors, directors, singers, comedians, and movie FX artists are just a few of the people who work in the business of keeping people entertained. Agriculture is another industry, as well as retail (Barnes & Noble, Home Goods, Wal-Mart, etc.), insurance, chemicals, nuclear weaponry, toys, fitness devices, the list goes on and on.

Most people aren't even aware of a fraction of all the industries in the economy. Therefore, they miss out on all sorts of awesome opportunities to make bank. I'll bet you never heard of "domaining" until I mentioned it a few paragraphs ago. Another example is my aunt's friend, who is a closet organizer. She literally helps rich people in New York City rotate their clothes in their closets as the seasons change! Who even knew that was a job?

And then within all of these industries, there are sub-industries and more sub-industries within those! For example, look at restaurants. There are food suppliers. There are companies that make and sell waitstaff uniforms. There are companies that specialize in printing restaurant menus. There are furniture companies that supply tables and chairs. There are people who come in and clean the restaurant at the end of the night. In fact, my aunt and uncle own a business that does just that - cleans restaurants and office buildings.

As you can see, there's a whole lot more money-making opportunity than just selling lemonade and walking dogs. You should deliberately learn about all industries. Sure, you could start reading *Forbes* magazine and *The Wall Street Journal* like a total nerd, but here are a couple things you could do that are a lot easier and also helpful.

One, ask every grown-up you meet what they do for a living. Two, every time you walk by a building in town, stop and try to figure out what business they're in. Do these simple things over time, and I guarantee you'll uncover far more lucrative opportunities on your *Kid Trillionaire* journey.

Volunteer

> *"You can have everything in life you want, if you will just help enough other people get what they want." - Zig Ziglar*

It can be hard to start making money as a kid. Grown-ups just don't take us seriously. I already told you how my uncle didn't hire me to build him a website, and he ended up paying 20 times what I would have charged to someone else - an adult, no doubt. Remember, you're always going to face obstacles and rejection. So how can a budding *Kid Trillionaire* ever make money if they're constantly dismissed because of their age and lack of experience?

Work for free! Just like how ice cream parlors give you free samples, once skeptical fossils experience your product or service, and you establish your competence, they'll become comfortable hiring you.

When my sister meets with a new piano student, she gives the first lesson for free. When I got my first podcast editing client, I produced not just one, but three episodes for free! And I spent over 40 hours working on them and learning all about Adobe Audition - which is super complicated - before I was able to prove my worth. I've had that client for nearly two years now, and I've made a lot of money from him. So it was definitely worth volunteering my services to start out.

Doing something for someone for free is a great way to grow your business, because it gains you valuable experience, testimonials, and new customers. So don't worry about giving away something for free, Scrooge Junior.

Maximize Time

"Either you run the day or the day runs you." - Jim Rohn

Here are four tips for making the most out of your precious time.

One, don't waste it. Ever. Like if you're on a road trip, and you're on one of those long and boring stretches, don't just stare out a window. Read a business book! And if you get carsick, listen to an audiobook or a podcast. Do the same while waiting at the dentist's office and for food in a restaurant. You get the idea.

Two, always work off a to-do list. Tim Ferriss famously always has his on a single sheet of paper folded up in his back pocket. Try to knock off your most important task first. If you aren't sure what that is, it's probably the most difficult thing that you've been avoiding.

Three, eliminate distractions. Think about it. If you were studying for a test, you might lock the door, turn off the TV, put your fidget spinner away... So do the same thing when you're trying to make money. Distractions are lethal because they kill your momentum, and it can take up to 20 minutes to get back on track. For more on this, read *Deep Work* by Cal Newport.

Four, "batch" and multitask when you can. When you go for a run, make sure you listen to a podcast or something. If you're going to your sister's soccer game, maybe you could bring some stuff to sell.

In order to maximize your money, you have to maximize your time.

Invest in Yourself

> *"The best investment you can make is in yourself." - Warren Buffett*

Congratulations! You've probably already done this by buying this book - or at least your parents did. I just wanted to let you know that you should never think twice about making an investment in yourself. Never hesitate to spend money on an experience, a course, a resource, a book, a technology, a tool, an experiment, or anything that you're certain will help you become a *Kid Trillionaire.*

It's so important to invest in yourself....you should even take on debt to increase your arsenal of marketable skills. Remember, big companies are constantly borrowing to plant seeds for future profits.

CHAPTER 13

NEXT ~~STEPS~~ LEAPS

> *"Anything can be achieved in small, deliberate steps. But there are times you need the courage to take a great leap; you can't cross a chasm in two small jumps." - David Lloyd George*

Great! You know why you should get rich and how to get rich. And I'm sure you're excited to get going. So what now?

Read *Kid Trillionaire* Again!

Did you just finish this book? Read it again immediately to reinforce the ideas and fire yourself up. Also, buy a copy of this book for your friends. They'll really appreciate it - so will I.

Get Serious

> *"A real decision is measured by the fact that you've taken a new action. If there's no action, you haven't truly decided." - Tony Robbins*

You're not going to ever become a *Kid Trillionaire* if your heart isn't into it. Reading this book is just the beginning of your journey.

Get Ready

> *"Before everything else, getting ready is the secret of success." - Henry Ford*

Whether you're planning on babysitting or selling golf balls at the local course, you have to do some preparation. Calculate prices, order inventory, contemplate ideas, make posters, create an Ebay account, do whatever it is you need to do to get ready.

Get Started

> *"A journey of a ~~thousand miles~~ trillion dollars begins with a single step." - ~~Lao Tzu~~ John Louzonis*

Now that you're serious and ready, it's time to begin. Put some of your old toys on Craigslist or Ebay for sale. Offer to petsit for your neighbor. Load up your backpack with candy to sell at school tomorrow. Knock on some doors and let the world know you are open for business.

Get Help

> *"If you want to go fast, go alone. If you want to go far, go with others." - African proverb*

Recruit your mom and dad, ask your friends, or con your little brother. Put your dog to work, if you can. Borrow money from your grandparents or your rich aunt if you have to. Your natural support network is already rooting for you and invested in your success so don't be shy to ask for a lot of help.

Get Going

> *"The path to success is to take massive, determined action."*
> *- Tony Robbins*

When you're starting out, it's okay to take baby steps. But if you want to become a *Kid Trillionaire*, you will have to ramp up your intensity level fast. It might sound like "work" but trust me, once the dough starts coming in....it will be pure FUN and more than worth the effort.

Join Me at KidsGetRich.com!

To learn how I got my first client at age 10, how I wrote this book, for more money-making resources, and the most recent updates on my personal *Kid Trillionaire* journey, go to KidsGetRich.com!

AFTERWORD

You must be wondering how a 13 year-old kid wrote a masterpiece like this. Well, it was tough. It took about 4 months to write the first draft, and 2 months to edit it. One of the guides I used to write this book is *Publish a Book and Grow Rich* by Gerry Robert. You can find a copy on Ebay.

Gerry's method is basically to write a list of the chapters you want in your book. Once you've done that, come up with 10-15 "subtopics" for each chapter. Then, write each subtopic. It's pretty easy once you get clear about your structure and into a rhythm.

When I was writing this book, I was about a third of the way through when I realized I was going too slowly. So I declared, in front of a whole bunch of people at my Dad's business mastermind meeting, that I was going to finish the first draft of this book in three months. And I did! As Nolan Bushnell, the creator of Atari (ask your parents) and Chuck E. Cheese said,

"The deadline is the ultimate inspiration."

Visit EinsteinBlueprint.com/John

As for the parents who I know are reading this, check out my Dad's website through the link above. It's all about how moms and dads can unleash their kids' full potential. Note that most of what you see on his websites....is my coding and web design work!

I want to thank you for reading this book. I hope you found it extremely profitable. Please send me all your success stories at my personal email address, john.louzonis@gmail.com.

Good luck!

John Louzonis
Manhattan, New York

KidsGetRich.com

APPENDIX: MY FAVORITE TOOLS

Book List

Dotcom Secrets by Russell Brunson. All ages! This is a fantastic book on marketing and selling online, but it will help you with those subjects in general.

The Millionaire Fastlane and *Unscripted* by M.J. DeMarco. Ages 13+ Both of these are absolutely amazing, but they may not be age-appropriate.

The Richest Man in Babylon by George Clason. All ages! This is a classic book that has helped many people make money.

The Magic of Believing by Claude Bristol. All ages! This is great book, and it teaches the power of believing in yourself. A must-read.

The Millionaire Next Door by Thomas Stanley. All ages! This is a classic book that tells you the little-known secrets of millionaires across the country.

The Four-Hour Workweek by Tim Ferriss. Ages 14+ This is only for teenagers. Seriously. But it can and will transform your life and blow your mind.

Any book written by Dan Kennedy is fantastic. Ages 14+

Those are just a couple books. There are many, many more on my website.

Resource List

Evan Carmichael's YouTube channel is fantastic.

Caleb Maddix also has an awesome YouTube channel.

EOFire podcast by John Lee Dumas.

SmartPassiveIncome.com

Udemy.com

Investopedia.com

Codecademy.com (Learn how to code for free!)

Adobe Creative Cloud

There are tons of resources and tools out there, and most of them are FREE. You'd be brain-dead to not to take advantage of them.

Made in the USA
Columbia, SC
12 July 2018